D0174840

JAN 0 2 2004

INTELLIGENCE:
THE HUMAN FACTOR

|SECURING THE NATION|

ISSUES IN AMERICAN NATIONAL SECURITY SINCE 9/11

Intelligence: The Human Factor

Maritime and Port Security

Narcotics and Terrorism

Intelligence:
The Human Factor

Col. W. Patrick Lang
U.S. Army (Ret.)

Series Consulting Editor
Larry C. Johnson
CEO, BERG Associates, LLC
Washington, D.C.

CHELSEA HOUSE
P U B L I S H E R S
A Haights Cross Communications Company

Philadelphia

CHELSEA HOUSE PUBLISHERS
VP, NEW PRODUCT DEVELOPMENT   Sally Cheney
DIRECTOR OF PRODUCTION   Kim Shinners
CREATIVE MANAGER   Takeshi Takahashi
MANUFACTURING MANAGER   Diann Grasse

Staff for INTELLIGENCE: THE HUMAN FACTOR
EDITOR   Patrick Stone
PRODUCTION EDITOR   Megan Emery
PHOTO EDITOR   Sarah Bloom
SERIES AND COVER DESIGNER   Keith Trego
LAYOUT   21st Century Publishing and Communications, Inc.

A Haights Cross Communications ◄┣ Company

www.chelseahouse.com

First Printing

1 3 5 7 9 8 6 4 2

Library of Congress Cataloging-in-Publication Data applied for.

ISBN 0-7910-7616-4

CONTENTS

Editor's Note

The terrorist attack of September 11 took the United States totally by surprise. It dispelled the illusion of an invulnerable nation, and the fallout has been felt in every sector of American society. A wounded, defensive, and wary nation has scrambled to find ways of preventing such attacks from ever happening again.

The United States is vast, diverse, and complex, though, and technological advances have made it even more difficult to maintain national security. Terrorist groups can communicate instantly with their own members and with other groups, and attacks can be timed to the second. Digital technology has made it easier to forge documents that establish identity. "Dirty bombs" and biological and chemical agents can be used to harm thousands of people at a time, and it is not always easy to detect them. The government's methods of tracking and dealing with these threats are also constantly evolving, and nowhere has the evolution been more marked than in the security community.

As Larry C. Johnson suggests in his introduction, the September 11 attack exploited weaknesses in American national security—particularly the lack of interagency communication. In October of 2001, President George W. Bush created the Department of Homeland Security to reduce the communication gaps; and since then, the network of security organizations has been recast as a more integrated and effective whole. As the Department has grown, all agencies involved have undergone major changes in structure and mission.

Before September 11, 2001, such changes would have meant little to American citizens; terrorism was considered a problem found in other countries, and the United States, with its advanced technologies and unparalleled military, was believed to be impervious to attack. Few people discussed national security beyond its effect on civil liberties. It was someone else's problem. The damage to the Pentagon and the destruction of the Twin Towers changed all that. The attack made national security *everyone's* problem; now, perhaps for the first time, American citizens are thinking about the nation's safety as an issue that affects them personally. Americans want and need to know about the people who protect them.

But, albeit for very good reasons, the field of national security is notoriously obscure. It can be difficult for the uninitiated even to name the agencies involved—far more difficult to understand them. What do we mean by "national security," and how has the concept evolved since September 11? What needs to be secured, and from whom, and what agencies are charged with securing it? How have the structures, functions, and mandates of these agencies changed since the attack? How can we prevent such attacks from happening again?

The goal of SECURING THE NATION is to pose these questions to the people best qualified to answer them—experts who have spent their careers promoting and protecting American national security. The authors treat their subjects thoroughly and authoritatively while making every effort to discuss complex issues in a way that is accessible to the lay reader. It is our hope that this series will foster the awareness that has become so vitally important in the post–9/11 world—where national security can no longer be seen as someone else's problem.

Introduction

The horrific attacks of September 11 changed forever our generation's sense of security. Although terrorism is not a new phenomenon, most Americans thought of terrorism as something that showed up in Hollywood movies. International terrorists rarely carried out attacks inside the United States. We were complacent.

When the first plane hit the northern tower of the World Trade Center, our complacency vanished. We now understand in some measure what our grandparents and great-grandparents felt when Pearl Harbor was attacked. We have felt firsthand the shock, bewilderment, confusion, and fear that they certainly felt upon hearing that the U.S. Navy's fleet at Pearl Harbor was bombed on Sunday morning, December 7, 1941.

Our own "date which will live in infamy," however, was more traumatic—not because more people died, but because we all witnessed the terrible events. Unlike our grandparents, most of whom learned of Pearl Harbor through secondhand sources—the radio or newspapers—we saw it happen live and, initially, unfiltered. We shared part of the experience of the people who were actually at or near the World Trade Center or the Pentagon on that fateful morning. Everyone who was near a television witnessed the burning buildings, the collapsing towers, and the fleeing crowds. We did not have to *imagine* fear, for we *saw* it.

The shock of the event was accompanied in short order by an overwhelming sense of vulnerability and the start of a search for how this could happen. Fear remained a dominant emotion. Images of troops in the streets in Washington, D.C., and New York City and combat air patrols by jet fighters reinforced the impression that we were under siege. Rather than venture out of the house, many stayed home. Airports and train stations were vacant. Business travel and tourism dropped precipitously.

In the succeeding months we have become acquainted with color-coded threat systems and witnessed the creation of new government institutions, such as the Transportation Security Agency and the Department of Homeland Security.

September 11 transformed America and its citizens. As the shock subsided and we coped with our fears, our attention shifted to explaining how the attack had been accomplished, punishing those responsible, and fixing the vulnerabilities that had enabled the attack to succeed. Americans—citizens and pundits alike—began asking questions: What would it take to make the United States truly secure? Is security a realistic objective, or are we chasing an illusion? What is the nature of the threat or threats that we are confronting? To stop religious extremists, are we willing to empower the federal government to spy on churches, mosques, or synagogues? How can we achieve effective national security and still remain a free people?

The books in SECURING THE NATION may not provide complete answers to these questions; some questions probably cannot be answered at all. But these books *will* equip the reader with knowledge about the security changes that are currently under way in the United States and will enable the reader to think and speak intelligently about issues of national security.

We are living in a historical moment, a period of time during which an event or series of events sets in motion forces that will shape the future, the world of the next generation. The bombing of Pearl Harbor, the Holocaust, the destruction of Hiroshima and Nagasaki by atomic bombs, the assassination of President John F. Kennedy in November of 1963—all were historical moments. The terrorist attack of September 11 and the invasion of Iraq both are historical moments. We are living in the midst of changes that years from now will be viewed by our children or grandchildren as watershed events.

COULD 9/11 HAVE BEEN PREVENTED?

Were the 9/11 hijackings an unexpected "bolt from the blue"? No, not really. Even though most Americans were unfamiliar with Osama bin Laden, Al Qaeda, and the radical Islamic terrorist training camps in Afghanistan, the intelligence community and the law enforcement community were well aware of these threats. Have you ever tried to put together a jigsaw puzzle? If you have the pieces of the puzzle, you can assemble the picture with concerted effort. If pieces are missing, the puzzle will be impossible to complete. In the aftermath of 9/11 we discovered that we'd had the clues all along, that information on the threat posed by bin Laden and his followers had been collected—but that those clues had been scattered among different government agencies and organizations. The agencies had not shared their puzzle pieces with one another.

A more specific example of this "failure to communicate" can be found in the Bojinka plot of 1995. In January of that year, Philippine police and firefighters accidentally stumbled upon a group of terrorists trying to make explosives in their apartment in downtown Manila. The subsequent investigation revealed that this group included one Abdul Basit, the man who had planned and carried out the first bombing of the World Trade Center in February of 1993. Basit managed to elude the Philippine police, but one of his partners, Hakim Murad, was arrested. When Murad was interrogated by Philippine police he revealed that he, Basit, and three others had planned to plant bombs on commercial jets and blow them up in mid-flight. The conspirators had intended to execute their plot, which they had codenamed "Bojinka," toward the end of that same January.

This information was passed to the Federal Bureau of Investigation (FBI), which was assisting the investigation. The FBI considered as its mission to gather evidence that could ultimately be presented before a judge and jury in order to convict the terrorists—not to share this information with other agencies. Neither did the FBI feel that it had a responsibility to warn American air carriers about the possible attack. Many FBI agents involved with the case believed that sharing this information would compromise the FBI's case and prevent the prosecution of the terrorist in custody.

Meanwhile, Central Intelligence Agency (CIA) operatives in Manila discovered the Bojinka plot and published an intelligence report. The report was then disseminated throughout Washington agencies and departments, including the Department of State, the Department of Defense, and the Federal Aviation Administration (FAA). This CIA report sparked a dispute among the agencies over whether to inform the American air carriers about the threat; at a meeting convened in late January, representatives from the various departments argued heatedly over what to do with this information. The FBI feared that releasing the information to the airlines would compromise its ability to prosecute the terrorists who had hatched the plot and was therefore strongly against sharing. For the State Department and the FAA, the goal was to use intelligence to warn the airliners about a threat and to take steps to prevent the attack. Thus the FBI was pitted against the State Department, the FAA, and the CIA; ultimately the decision was made to warn the airlines. No attack is known to have occurred.

This story of the discovery of the Bojinka plot and the

uphill battle to share the information obtained from the investigation illustrates the processes and bureaucratic cultures that allowed 9/11 to happen. I am not assigning blame or fault to any particular organization. Rather, I want to emphasize that although we have one government, it is made up of a variety of departments and agencies, each of which has a unique way of looking at the world. It is possible for each department to work to the best of its ability to do its job properly but, in the end, only help to create a disaster. The law enforcement mentality sees its task as one of acquiring and preserving evidence with the ultimate goal of convicting a suspect in a court of law. The work of a criminal investigation is compartmented—in other words, only those directly involved with the case will have access to the evidence collected. Given that an organization like the FBI conducts thousands of criminal investigations every year, it becomes easy to appreciate that no one person or group of persons can fully understand the various cases being pursued.

In the aftermath of 9/11, we learned more disturbing facts. An FBI office in Minnesota had tried unsuccessfully in August of 2001 to obtain a subpoena to examine a computer used by Zaccarias Moussai, who was taking flying lessons but had shown no interest in learning to perform takeoffs or landings. Earlier in 2001, the FBI office in Arizona had submitted a request to investigate foreign Muslims who were taking flying lessons and acting suspiciously. This request also had been rejected. Then we learned that the FBI's debriefing of Hakim Murad in January 1995 had revealed that the terrorists had planned to hijack commercial airliners in the United States and fly them into CIA headquarters—and we came to the sickening realization that we'd had key clues in our hands and had not understood them or acted on them. Many law enforcement agents had recognized the potential threat, but their efforts to attract attention to the information had been blocked by bureaucratic procedures and also by individuals who had not appreciated the magnitude of the threat.

The intelligence community failed to process the clues and act in time to prevent the attack; here again, as with the example of the FBI, we have learned that there was plenty of information available. In January of 2001, for example, CIA officers in Malaysia monitored a meeting that included individuals who later hijacked the planes on 9/11. The CIA claims its agents passed this information to the FBI, but it appears that the intelligence was sent through an informal e-mail. In order to be taken seriously, information sent between agencies must be sent in the proper format. In this case, the informal nature of the communication resulted in the information's "falling between the cracks."

From the perspective of the intelligence community, it is important to protect information in order to hide the identity of the sources. Unlike the FBI, which is focused on collecting evidence to build a specific case, the intelligence community generates volumes of more general information. Genuine intelligence analysts are paid to sift through the information flood and to extract important data, much like a gold prospector who crouches over a stream for hours at a time, filtering out mud and water to find the occasional nugget of gold. But the task is greater than just *collecting* the information; the pieces of intelligence must also be assembled, analyzed, interpreted, and molded into a coherent story.

The ability of CIA and FBI analysts to predict or even fully analyze terrorist threats has been restricted, however, by limitations on the kinds of intelligence these agencies can collect and analyze. In the 1960s and early 1970s, President Nixon ordered the FBI and the CIA to gather information about his political enemies, and these abuses led to reforms that prevented the FBI from collecting intelligence on American citizens without evidence of a possible crime. The reforms also limited the CIA's ability to operate domestically; consequently, the powers of the CIA and FBI to conduct domestic intelligence activities were scaled back dramatically. Since then, the CIA has focused its attention and resources on threats outside the United States, and the FBI has emphasized building specific cases for prosecution. In the years before 9/11, no agency or department of the United States government had the power to collect and analyze intelligence about terrorist activities *within* the United States that were being directed by *foreign-based* entities.

The problem of information sharing between the FBI and the CIA becomes even more profound once we understand that the law enforcement community and the intelligence community both comprise multiple agencies. The law enforcement community, for example, includes the U.S. Customs Service, the Drug Enforcement Administration (DEA), the Internal Revenue Service (IRS), the Secret Service, the U.S. Marshals, the Bureau of Alcohol, Tobacco, Firearms, and Explosives (ATF), and the U.S. Park Police. Each agency has the power to conduct federal criminal investigations, and no central system exists to organize all the information the agencies collect. In fact, there have been numerous instances in which multiple agencies pursued the same target. In 1991, for instance, DEA agents arrested Dandeny Muñoz ("La Quika") Mosquera for drug trafficking and money laundering. Mosquera, who had planned the bombing of an Avianca commercial airplane in Colombia in November of 1989, also was the target of an terrorist investigation led by the FBI. Rather than cooperate in the investigation, the two federal agencies pursued the target independently, with DEA winning the race.

The intelligence community, though not as large, is equally diverse. In addition to the CIA, there is the Defense Intelligence Agency (DIA), the National Security Agency (NSA), the National Reconnaissance Office (NRO), various intelligence outfits in the

U.S. military's regional commands, the Department of Energy (DOE), and the FAA. The CIA, DIA, NSA, and NRO specialize in intelligence collection, which means they use either human spies or technology to intercept signals. Once this information is obtained, it is turned into a finished product, much like a newspaper article, and distributed to policymakers and intelligence analysts in other organizations. In highly sensitive cases, however, there is some information that is not shared with other organizations.

The law enforcement and intelligence communities both knew that Osama bin Laden and his followers were responsible for previous attacks and were planning future attacks. Unfortunately, the hunt for bin Laden and the effort to prevent future attacks were neither coordinated nor focused: Each organization pursued the target using its own resources and according to its own goals. In the mid-1990s, for instance, the government of the Republic of the Sudan offered to hand bin Laden over to American authorities. The offer was handled primarily by the Department of Justice and the Department of State, rather than through a "full-court" effort by the entire government. According to one of those involved in brokering the potential deal, it fell apart over the fact that no one at the Justice Department believed a solid, prosecutable case could be brought against bin Laden based on the evidence available at that time.

After 9/11, we learned that there were numerous serious indicators of an impending attack but that the information had been scattered among too many agencies to form a meaningful picture. Parts of the Al Qaeda network had even been penetrated by the U.S. government, but we had failed to pay attention to available intelligence and to act on it in a decisive, coordinated way.

Thus there were *two* important failures that paved the way for 9/11—not only the failure to share information between the intelligence community and the law enforcement community, but also a failure of analysis. We had the key pieces of the puzzle, but we failed to put them together. Because of these twin failures, the Twin Towers collapsed, the Pentagon was partially burned, and a plane fell in a Pennsylvania field after valiant passengers struggled to wrest control of the aircraft from its hijackers.

PUNISHING THOSE RESPONSIBLE

The terrorist attack of September 11 awakened the slumbering United States from years of apathy. We discovered in early 1995 that Osama bin Laden was linked to the terrorists who had bombed the World Trade Center in 1993. With attacks by Islamic militants against the U.S. military's housing complex in Dharan, Saudi Arabia, and the August 1998 bombings of the American embassies in Kenya and Tanzania, it became clear that we were at war with bin Laden. Bin Laden and his followers, who were based in Afghanistan, were training warriors for *jihad*—Islamic holy war against Western infidels—and plotting new offensives. President Clinton launched cruise missile strikes against Al Qaeda training facilities in August of 1998, but the missile strikes inflicted little damage on the terrorists. When they attacked the U.S.S. *Cole* off the coast of Yemen in October of 2000, the United States did nothing. The terrorists considered the United States a weak nation, one incapable of defending itself.

It was not until nineteen Islamic militants simultaneously attacked the nation on September 11 that the United States found the motivation to mount a significant response. President Bush and his national-security team immediately began to plan the nation's strategy. The immediate problem was the terrorist training camps in Afghanistan, so within days U.S. intelligence and special-operations personnel were on the ground in that country. They forged ties with opponents of the

Taliban, the main regime that was harboring bin Laden and his Al Qaeda followers. Two months after the attack of September 11, U.S. military operations were under way in Afghanistan, successfully routing both the Taliban and Al Qaeda.

The success of the war in Afghanistan proved to be the first and least difficult phase in the "war on terror." Not only were the training camps destroyed, but American forces captured Islamic radicals, documents, and computers that in turn provided law enforcement and intelligence with an information bonanza. Unlike previous failed efforts, the FBI and CIA now joined forces to work together in genuine partnership. An interagency team established operations centers throughout the upper floors of the J. Edgar Hoover Building, the FBI's headquarters, which sits six blocks east of the White House. In addition to FBI agents, the task forces were staffed by representatives from U.S. Customs, the Department of the Treasury, the ATF, the IRS, the Secret Service, the U.S. Marshals, the NSA, the CIA, the DOE, and the NRO. It was a veritable "alphabet soup" of government agencies and an important attempt at cooperation.

With the destruction of Al Qaeda training camps in Afghanistan, the number of viable military targets for counter-terrorist operations decreased dramatically. As a result, the focus shifted to intelligence and law enforcement operations, both domestic and international The investigation of Al Qaeda revealed a multilayered organization with support cells and adherents in numerous countries. Working with foreign police and intelligence operatives, U.S. agents set to work in hundreds of regions around the world. Financial investigations revealed covert support to terrorist operations from Islamic charities based in the United States. Other terrorists were caught engaging in more mundane criminal activities, such as cigarette smuggling.

The capture of key members of Al Qaeda provided further

leads in the search for additional collaborators. A few of those apprehended were subjected to conventional arrest, and many more are being held in military detention centers. Since 9/11, the United States has entered new legal territory in several domains, among which is prisoners' rights. The terrorists in custody are treated humanely according to the standards of the Geneva Convention, but they are denied the legal rights granted to prisoners of war. By removing the terrorists from society, the United States has disrupted their ability to plan new attacks, recruit new followers, and kill more innocent civilians; it is no coincidence that in 2002 international terrorist attacks fell to their lowest level in 34 years.

FIXING THE VULNERABILITIES

The lack of information sharing between and among government agencies and the failure to act on information in our possession were not the only shortcomings that the 9/11 attack revealed. In the aftermath, we finally acknowledged that many of our security systems were inadequate and under-funded. For example, the hijackings were *not* a consequence of inadequate work by security screeners; in fact, the security companies that guarded the screening checkpoints at Logan and Dulles Airports did their job properly and permitted on the aircraft only items that were acceptable by existing security standards. Before September 12, 2001, modeling knives were allowed aboard commercial airliners.

The Al Qaeda terrorists did not defeat the aviation security systems that were in place on September 11 so much as exploit the gaps in those systems. Although not heavily armed, the terrorists ensured that at least four members of their group were aboard each plane. They selected domestic flights with the full understanding that international flights would be more likely to be guarded by air marshals. They also knew that they did not *have* to be heavily armed. They could hijack a plane simply by announcing an intention to do so and threatening the pilots, flight attendants, and passengers—brandishing even something as innocuous as a fountain pen or a cylindrical tube.

The aviation security system of the time was based on the belief that even if someone hijacked a plane by threatening to detonate a bomb, the crew, especially the pilots, would stay in control of the plane because hijackers were not pilots. September 11 exposed this as false. Not only had some of the hijackers undergone training as pilots, but they also were suicidal—preserving their own lives was *not* among their goals.

The flight crews on 9/11 acted in accordance with their training. They did their jobs bravely. Pilots and flight attendants had been taught to handle hijackers in much the way that a bank teller is taught to deal with a bank robber—to cooperate, to surrender what the aggressor wants, and to stall as much as possible in the hope that reinforcements will arrive. On 9/11 we learned the hard way that this training was not a valid way of handling a modern hijacking—and that fuel-filled planes could very easily be transformed into human-controlled cruise missiles.

Since the 9/11 hijackings, the federal government has been taking concrete steps to prevent such a thing from ever happening again. Aboard the commercial airliners, there was a fundamental shift in the ways in which flight crews were taught to respond to a hijacking. Rather than cooperating and granting hijackers access to the cockpit, pilots now remain behind a locked door. The doors have been hardened to withstand, albeit temporarily, attempts to open them, even those attempts that use bullets or hand grenades. A hardened door buys the pilots time; with luck, the extra time will enable them to take the aircraft down to an altitude that will minimize the risk of a catastrophic decompression if the skin of the aircraft is breached. In addition, pilots now are authorized to carry a pistol and have the last-resort option of being able to open a lockbox, remove a handgun, and defend the plane from being taken over if a hijacker succeeds in bypassing the door.

Significant changes in aviation security have also occurred on the ground. The responsibility for security screening has been taken away from private contractors and put into the hands of the U.S. government's new Transportation Security Agency. Money has been appropriated to purchase and deploy explosive-detection systems to check luggage for bombs. Passengers traveling by air today have a much greater guarantee that the trip will be safe and more secure.

Improving aviation security was relatively easy because a "roadmap" for the process already existed. Previous reports issued under both Republican and Democratic administrations—the *Report of the President's Commission on Aviation Security and Terrorism* (1990) and the *White House Commission Report on Aviation Safety and Security* (1997) had identified the problems and recommended solutions.

But securing the nation is not a simple proposition, and there is no easy "roadmap." America's sense of vulnerability was magnified by 9/11 and by the wave of anthrax attacks that followed it—which remain unexplained even now. Regardless of the cause, the spate of infections highlighted the fact that the existing system for handling and delivering postal mail did not include safeguards or systems for detecting and preventing the movement of hazardous materials. The federal government responded rapidly by installing equipment to detect and disinfect suspicious mail. Also, new measures were adopted for improving communications with local public-health departments and the Centers for Disease Control and Prevention (CDC), the main federal institution charged with protecting the public from disease.

Out of this chaos, the Bush administration conceived of a

broader vision of national security. In a move that recalls the National Security Act of 1948, which led to the creation of the Department of Defense and the Central Intelligence Agency, the Bush administration proposed establishing what it called the Department of Homeland Security. This federal department would consist of agencies drawn from the Department of the Treasury (e.g., the Secret Service, the U.S. Customs Service), the Department of Justice (e.g., the Immigration and Naturalization Service), the Department of Transportation (e.g., the Coast Guard, the Federal Aviation Administration), and the Department of Energy. In theory, the new department would provide any administration with the ability to establish a clear security budget for protecting the nation. This reorganization also would reduce the overlap in agency activities and enable the federal government to focus scarce resources on specific problems.

With the arrival of the Department of Homeland Security comes a central mechanism for dealing with a variety of security tasks that previously were dealt with in a haphazard, uncoordinated way. The responsibility for ensuring that there are plans and standards for protecting nuclear power plants, seaports, public transportation (including buses, subways, and commuter trains), public water systems, and electrical grids is now fairly straightforward. This does not mean that the task is simple, though. The Department of Homeland Security represents a collection of agencies and personnel, and the difficulty of managing it will rival the challenge of managing the Department of Defense.

Less dramatic but equally important reforms are under way at the CIA and the FBI, the FBI's transformation being the greater of the two. Before 9/11, for example, documents and records that the FBI obtained in the course of a criminal investigation would lie dormant in boxes; they were never converted to electronic files that could be searched using current data mining technology. Under the leadership of Robert Mueller, the FBI has established a unit on the top floor of its headquarters, the J. Edgar Hoover Building, that is dedicated to scanning the millions of documents that the agency collects. The database resulting from this scanning effort is large already and growing. It offers to investigators a previously unavailable resource for finding links between terrorists and mundane criminals. In addition, the FBI has set up several different task force operation centers that are staffed around the clock and include representatives from other agencies.

President Bush also directed the FBI and the CIA to create a joint threat-monitoring and threat-assessment center. Both agencies initially resisted this plan, but both relented under persistent pressure from the president and his advisors. Providing one place where threat information from domestic and international sources can be evaluated cooperatively and analyzed for links will bridge the gap that enabled critical warning intelligence to go unnoticed in the weeks and months prior to 9/11.

CONCLUSION

The books in SECURING THE NATION provide a comprehensive introduction to the changes that have taken place in American national security since the terrorist attack of September 11. The current issues in national security are discussed by experts who have worked extensively to resolve those issues. Certainly, there is nothing wrong with an academic viewpoint—but theoreticians who have no grounding in practice often have difficulty in finding the roots of the issues they study. The authors in this series, in contrast, are thoughtful practitioners. They have served their country as military officers and government officials. They have grappled with the problems of developing and implementing new policies amid intense bureaucratic battles. Some have been sent on top-secret missions by presidents—many of which remain highly classified.

As you read and debate the information in these books, I encourage you to think critically. The publication of a piece of information does not make that information true. Be quick to ask why, and insist on hard, empirical evidence to corroborate or refute a statement claimed as fact. Hopefully, you will discover that national security is not based on deploying the most technologically sophisticated metal detector or hiring thousands of new specialists—but on freedom and the rule of law. The freedoms we enjoy belong to citizens who know their rights and understand how their government works.

The surprise attack on Pearl Harbor in 1941 produced a reaction of fear, a fear that ultimately was invoked to justify confiscating the property of Japanese Americans and jailing them in concentration camps. Even though the United States was at war with Germany and Italy as well as Japan, the federal government targeted only citizens of Japanese heritage, possibly because they were the most "different." The September 11 hijackers were Islamic radicals from Saudi Arabia and Egypt, so 9/11 created a similar opportunity to target Arab Americans. The Bush administration made a conscious effort after 9/11 to ensure that Arab Americans were not defined as a threat, so the nation was not subjected to another episode of internment or widespread persecution. But the analogy illustrates the need for citizens to understand issues of national security: Lapses in security can and *have* been used to justify restricting the civil liberties of American citizens. Consider the ideas in these books, use them to build your understanding of the federal government's operations, and make the choice to play a constructive role in securing the nation.

Larry C. Johnson
CEO, BERG Associates, LLC
Washington, D.C.

1

Intelligence and Its Heroes

What is "intelligence?" It is the product and process of collection, processing, evaluation, and analysis of *information* concerning foreign countries, armed forces, or areas of interest. In other words, intelligence is about information. It has always been about information—the information needed by governments and armies to function in both peacetime and war. There is nothing new about the need for governments and leaders to have the best information that can be obtained to make sound decisions.

In the Bible, Moses sends twelve spies into Canaan to learn of the strengths and weaknesses of the enemies of the Hebrews (Numbers 13). Unfortunately for him, only two of the men sent on this mission return with useful information, and all the news is bad, as their enemies are shown to be very strong. After the death of Moses, Joshua, the new leader of the Hebrews, sends another group of spies into Canaan "to view the land and Jericho" (Joshua 2:1). (Joshua was one of the two successful spies of the previous mission, so we can guess that his experience with this kind of work made him believe that it will be useful.) This team returns with much better news: They report that the Canaanites are weak and afraid of the coming of the Hebrews. Based on this information and instructions from Jehovah, Joshua invades Canaan (which is now known as Israel).

During the American Revolutionary War (1775–1783), the British colonies in North America (later known as the United

States of America) fought a long and bitter struggle for independence from Great Britain that at times seemed hopeless and that would probably have ended in defeat for the colonists had it not been for France's help. In the middle of that war, General George Washington sent a twenty-year-old captain of Rangers behind the British front lines in New York to learn all he could about British strengths, weaknesses, and positions. Nathan Hale was that captain, and he was disguised as a schoolteacher. (This was easy for him because he had actually been a schoolteacher for a few years after graduating with honors from Yale University in 1773.) Hale was an admirable young man—intelligent, athletic, and liked by all who knew him. He was captured by the British Army and hanged as a spy before he could complete his mission, and the British authorities said that they regretted the necessity of his execution. International law has always held that spies should be punished with death. This is not because spying is dishonorable; it is because successful spies pose a very grave threat to a targeted army or country. On the scaffold, young Nathan Hale said that he regretted only that he had but one life to give for his country. His statue stands today

Espionage in the Civil War

The first large-scale espionage services created in the United States were brought into being during the Civil War (1861–1865). In this fratricidal conflict, America's bloodiest war, both the North and the South made extensive use of espionage and covert action organizations. Infiltration of Southern (Confederate) agents into the North was relatively easy for two reasons: first, that there were large numbers of Southern sympathizers in Maryland and Washington, D.C., and second, that the North had a policy of accepting all Southerners as loyal Americans if they signed an oath of allegiance. On the Northern (Union) side, early failures were redeemed in 1863 when Ulysses S. Grant became general in chief and employed Colonel George Sharp, an amateur soldier with a flair for organization and improvisation, to build an effective Union Army Intelligence Service. This agency served the United States well but did not survive the end of the war.

in front of the headquarters of the Central Intelligence Agency in Langley, Virginia, and on the campus of his alma mater, Yale University, in New London, Connecticut.

In the aftermath of World War II (1939–1945), the world found itself divided into two rival and hostile camps. The American and Soviet allies who had defeated Nazi Germany and imperial Japan together confronted each other across a divide of political ideology and economic philosophy so deep that it was never bridged during the long decades of the "Cold War" (1945–1990). This situation ended only when the Soviet Union disintegrated in 1991. At that time, the country simply fell apart under the weight of its failed economy and the financial burden involved in supporting military and foreign policy programs big enough to rival those of the United States. Nevertheless, for almost fifty years the two countries opposed each other across the world in a rivalry fraught with danger for all mankind because they were both armed with massive arsenals of nuclear and thermonuclear weapons and the aircraft and guided missiles needed to deliver them to targets in the enemy's homeland. At the height of the Cold War, each side possessed more than fifteen thousand such weapons, and it was officially estimated by the United States government that a Soviet surprise attack would result in a minimum of 40 million dead in the United States.

In this situation, foreign affairs, military preparedness, and detailed information of the "other side's" capabilities and intentions were taken very seriously by all the governments involved in the worldwide quarrel. For this reason vast amounts of money were spent on intelligence organizations, in the hope that good quality information would enable the opponent countries to avoid war or to survive war if it could not be avoided. In pursuit of this information "insurance policy," great intelligence services were built in the hope that institutionalizing the function of information gathering and analysis would ensure the quality of knowledge needed for decisions involving national survival.

In the Soviet Union, the intelligence function resided in the

KGB (in its original Russian, the Committee for State Security) and the GRU (Soviet military intelligence). The KGB was a civilian government bureaucracy, although members were assigned ranks that were similar to police ranks. The KGB had its roots in the tradition of the police-controlled society that had characterized tsarist Russia before the revolution of 1917—a revolution that created the communist government of the Soviet Union. Vladimir Ilyich Lenin, the founder of the Soviet state, continued this police-state tradition by constructing a Communist Party police agency charged with the protection of Communist rule in the new state. The founder of this agency was a man named Felix Dzerzhinsky, and the agency was known across the world as the "Cheka." And, ever after, Soviet intelligence men from this group were known as "Chekists." Over the seventy-odd years of the existence of the Soviet Communist state, the name of this organization changed several times. At first it was the All-Russian Extraordinary Commission for Combating Counterrevolution and Sabotage ("Vecheka" or "Cheka"). The People's Commissariat of Internal Affairs (NKVD) was formed in 1918. In 1922 came the State Political Directorate (GPU), which was subordinate to the NKVD; within a year this became the Unified State Political Directorate (OGPU), which was not. The agency was known as the Main (or Chief) Directorate for State Security (GUGB) beginning in 1934; its initals shifted to NKGB in 1941, MKB in 1946, and finally KGB in 1954. These name changes were caused by a restless need to reorganize that is common in large organizations, and they did not mean very much.

No matter what the name, the Cheka remained the group created by Dzerzhinsky and went on with its work of information and sedition. The group was so successful in protecting Communist rule in Russia that Lenin expanded its task to include intelligence gathering and subversion work in countries outside the Soviet Union. The KGB was very good at this work and specialized in the use of human sources (spies) to search out foreign secrets and to prepare other countries for the revolutions that the

Soviets hoped would bring an end to capitalist economies and liberal democracy everywhere in the world.

Because the "Chekists" were civilians and neither responsive nor competent in supporting the planning and war fighting needs of the Soviet military, the Soviets built a separate intelligence capability dedicated solely to the strategic information needs of their armed forces. The Communist Party of the Soviet Union ruled the KGB directly and directed its work into fields that dealt mainly with politics, economics, or foreign scientific "breakthroughs." The Soviet military needed specific information about potential adversaries' military strengths, organization, and plans. To fulfill these needs, a military intelligence group was created within the Soviet General Staff that was concerned solely with the information needs of the armed forces, without the additional burden of carrying out the revolutionary agenda of the Communist Party and larger Soviet government. This group was known by the initials "GRU," an acronym for the name of the Fourth Main Directorate of the Soviet General Staff.

In every country in the world, there is at least one civilian intelligence agency and another that is manned by, and is the property of, the military. Without exception, these organizations are deadly opponents and rivals for government favor and for the budget money that comes with such favor. The officers and operatives of these rival groups are seldom friends. The Soviet Union was no different, and as a result it was a rarity that individuals should have had careers that included assignments in both groups. It just did not happen, because the two groups did not trust each other.

An exception to this was the case of Colonel Oleg Penkovsky (1919–1963). Penkovsky was a career officer of the Soviet Army. He came from a military family. His father had been an officer of the army of imperial Russia before the Communist revolution of 1917. Oleg Penkovsky wanted to be an army officer from his boyhood. He was a Russian patriot, very intelligent, a good student, and a supporter of the Soviet government. Nevertheless, he had a great deal of trouble realizing his ambition in life. Because he came from a family of military officers under the previous government, he was considered to be a "class enemy" and potentially disloyal to the communists. If it had not been for World War II, during which the Soviet Union was very nearly destroyed by the attack of Nazi Germany, Penkovsky may never have been allowed to join his country's army as an officer. The German invasion of the Soviet Union in 1941 changed that, for the Germans might have achieved their goal of destroying the Soviet Union had it not been for the foolish and uninformed strategic decisions of the German dictator, Adolf Hitler. In desperation, the Soviet government allowed people whom it never would have tolerated in less dangerous times to become leaders in the Soviet Army. Penkovsky became a Soviet soldier and fought with distinction throughout the war, receiving several decorations for valor. At the end of the war, Penkovsky was chosen to become an officer of the GRU on the basis of his outstanding service record to the Soviet state. In preparation for this service, he was sent to attend the Military Diplomatic Academy in Moscow—the "prep school" of the GRU. He graduated with distinction. He was also sent to study at the Frunze Higher Military Academy, one of the most senior military schools for officers in his country. He then served as the military attaché in the Soviet Embassy in Ankara, Turkey, where he headed the GRU "station" in that country and spied on Turkish and American activities connected to Turkey's membership in the North Atlantic Treaty Organization (NATO). He was a big success in this new field and respected in the KGB for his loyalty and willingness to help that group in its overseas operations. By the time he returned to Moscow to be assigned to GRU headquarters, he was believed to be one of the most promising new officers of either service and to have a bright future in Soviet intelligence ahead of him. But this was not to be: In the course of his studies and intelligence work abroad, Colonel Penkovsky had become disillusioned with communism and its obvious drive for world domination. He also believed that the Soviet leader of his time, Nikita Khrushchev, was irresponsible and likely to cause a nuclear war.

In 1961, Penkovsky was sent to London, England, supposedly to head a "trade mission" but in reality to act as the head of a KGB spying team. In England, he contacted a British "businessman" whom he suspected of having connections to British intelligence and offered to help the West. He was correct in his assessment and held a meeting with British intelligence and another with the American Central Intelligence Agency (CIA). In these meetings, he managed to convince the British and Americans that he was sincere and they accepted his offer to help. He was to be a "double spy"—pretending to do Soviet espionage work (and helped in this by the British and Americans) while actually sending reports to the West about high-level Soviet activities.

Penkovsky did this for two years (1961–1962) in London and Moscow, delivering a wealth of photographs, drawings, written reports, and other material on Russia's military plans, goals, and espionage operations, its long-range missiles, and its space satellites. During the Cuban Missile Crisis (October 1962), he was able to tell President John F. Kennedy (1960–1963) that the Soviet missile forces were not prepared to go to war with the United States. It was on the basis of this information that Kennedy demanded the withdrawal of Soviet missiles from Cuba; Khrushchev backed down and removed them.

In 1963, Penkovsky was arrested in Moscow by the KGB, whose leadership probably had identified him through the evidence of a spy working for their agency in a Western government. He was tried for treason and espionage and executed by firing squad later that year.

Was he a traitor? He was certainly a traitor to the Soviet Union, but the situation is more complex than that simple judgment. In his mind, he no longer considered himself to be a Soviet citizen. He believed that he had given his allegiance to America and thus was serving his new homeland. The CIA assured him that he would be resettled with honor as an American army officer when his tenure as a spy was over. He said that he was interested in Florida—but he never had the chance to determine whether Miami Beach would have suited him. A brave soul who acted from conviction, he is an example of what in the world of clandestine intelligence is called a "walk-in"—that is, someone who takes personal action to attract the attention of an intelligence service and who volunteers his services. A great many intelligence "cases" begin in this way, and often they are among the best if the subject's motives are as genuine as those of poor Penkovsky.

These are just a few examples of the more illustrious intelligence operatives who affected history. They were difficult to select, for they are typical of so many others who have given so much to the causes in which they believed.

2

Collection in All Its Varieties

THE PROCESS OF INTELLIGENCE

Intelligence is sometimes thought of as an activity sporadically engaged in by the eccentrically gifted element to be found in any population. Many stories exist in accounts of British and American intelligence of the World War II period that stress the "freewheeling" quality of many of the operations and people of Allied intelligence in that war. In fact, the British secret services were full of the younger children of the aristocracy, men and women for whom the rigid conventions governing middle-class life were unfamiliar. These operatives tended to be unconventional, free-thinking, "outside the box" types who were not intimidated by the expectations of their bureaucratic superiors and for whom the war and their work were just a continuation of their "hunting and shooting" lives in the country. Indeed, many of their successes (and some of their failures) can be attributed to their penchant for unconventional behavior.

President Franklin D. Roosevelt (1933–1945) was a great admirer of such people. He was a northeastern aristocrat by background, character, and outlook, and it would be fair to say that he was an Anglophile. As a result, the Office of Strategic Services (OSS), an intelligence service that he constructed during the war, was closely modeled on the

British services and sought to recruit similar employees and military personnel. Throughout its existence, the OSS (1942–1946) filled its ranks with the graduates of elite "Ivy League" and similar institutions and did not hesitant to attempt schemes and operations that more typical Americans might have dismissed as "out of the question." The CIA was established in 1947 with the wartime experience of the OSS as an example of success and with many of the same people, individuals who found it difficult to adapt to a peacetime life after the excitement and adventure of war service. The process of turning this band of adventurers into a government bureaucracy that could survive in the environment of the perpetual inter-governmental struggle between departments for authority and budgeted money was a long and frustrating one. The early years (the 1950s and 1960s) were filled with misadventures and a mixed record of success against the enemies of the United States.

An example of this kind of unhappy experience that is often mentioned is the 1950s operation in which the CIA attempted to build guerrilla forces throughout the Soviet

The Birth of American Espionage

Before World War II, the United States possessed signals intelligence groups, staff analytic sections, and military and naval attachés through its Navy and War Departments—but the country had no real espionage capability. At the beginning of the war, President Franklin D. Roosevelt created the Office of Strategic Services (OSS). He asked Major General William ("Wild Bill") Donovan, a combat hero of World War I and a Wall Street lawyer, to study the British methods of fighting the intelligence war in Europe. In the end, Donovan and Roosevelt adopted the model of the British Special Operations Executive (SOE), a wartime covert-action unit brought into being by Winston Churchill, rather than the British Secret Intelligence Service (SIS), a four-hundred-year-old "pure" intelligence service.

Union that could undermine a possible Soviet attack on Western Europe by attacking the Soviet Union from the rear. Supplies and weapons were "cached" all over Eastern Europe and "stay-behind" teams established in Russia, Poland, and at other sites. This must have seemed like a good idea at the time, but in fact many of these operations were compromised and contaminated by the use of the West German "Gehlen Organization" that had been "inherited" by the U.S. occupation forces in Germany from the World War II German Army. The KGB heavily infiltrated this organization, and the stay-behind teams were rounded up and destroyed over a period of several years. This was a disaster that did nothing to build confidence in the CIA in its early years.

Another example of an early failure was the attempt to trigger a revolt against the Communist Castro government in Cuba in 1961. In this case, the CIA placed too much faith in the exaggerated claims of Cuban exiles in Florida who believed that most Cubans would rise in armed revolt against the government if there were any sort of landing by a Cuban liberation force. Against the advice of the Joint Chiefs of Staff (JCS), the CIA attempted the invasion. The small Cuban force was defeated and captured, and the American government looked foolish and ineffectual. Neither of these operations was, strictly speaking, "intelligence," for the plan involved armed warfare rather than information gathering and analysis, but the task *had* been given to the CIA—and the collapse of the plans hurt the image of intelligence generally.

The same could be said of the intelligence activities of the armed services. In spite of a long history in support of combat operations and strategic planning, the leadership of the armed forces was always unwilling to accept the institutional discipline and collective wisdom of the generals and admirals, and therefore, intelligence was of rather dubious value. American military intelligence has never carried the prestige and "cachet" that such work carries in many other countries' armed forces.

THE INTELLIGENCE CYCLE

To ensure that intelligence functions are carried out in an orderly and logical way, taking into account all relevant data and factors, the intelligence community (the "collective" of all the many federal government intelligence groups) decided long ago that a uniform system should be adopted for processing requests for information and the resulting "take." This carefully phased process is universally known as "the intelligence cycle." It has the following segments:

- requirements;

- collection;

- analysis; and

- dissemination or distribution of reports.

Intelligence is about satisfying the information needs of the "consumers" who may be either civilian elected or appointed policy makers or military officers in command of forces as at every level from Battalion Commander (600 soldiers) to Field Army or Fleet Commander (up to 300,000 soldiers). These information requirements are usually established by staff assistants of the supported commander or decision maker and sent to the intelligence collection agencies and units for action. These requirements sometimes are in the form of a directive or request letter or electronic message or, more commonly, in the case of military commands, in the form of Essential Elements of Information (EEI). The requirements can include all sorts of things. Some examples would be: enemy "order of battle" (the study of enemy strength), disposition, personalities, intentions, etc. Another kind of requirement from the political side of government would be a request for economic data showing the financial wealth of a possible opponent. A third example would be an expressed need to know the state of development of an adversary's advanced weapons (e.g., nuclear weapons).

In this book, though, we are concerned mostly with the second phase of the cycle: collection. At the national level, the means of collection available to a country like the United States are many and are very capable. The two primary routes with which we are concerned here are signals collection (SIGINT) and human-source intelligence (HUMINT).

SIGINT

SIGINT, or signals collection, is one kind of information collection that is much relied on by national authority. This form of collection involves intercepting other people's communications, as well as their noncommunications electronic signals, such as radar. The National Security Agency (NSA) is charged by law with this task, and to do the job, the NSA has more people and money given to it than any other agency of the intelligence community. Using satellite-based remote systems, as well as aircraft, ships, and ground stations, many thousands of civilian employees and military members are dedicated to this task. SIGINT is heavily relied upon by decision makers in the belief that an enemy will not normally lie to its own people in its own communications.

Imagery

Imagery is a crucial aspect of SIGINT—in particular, the analysis of photographs taken from above. Space satellites and aircraft belonging either to a national satellite reconnaissance organization or to a country's air force are routinely tasked to take the pictures that give an accurate view of enemy activity on the ground. A famous example of this occurred in October of 1962, when U-2 reconnaissance aircraft flown by U.S. Air Force pilots for the CIA discovered that the Soviet Union had placed intermediate-range ballistic missiles (IRBMs) in Cuba that could cover most of the southeastern United States.

Open-Source Research

Libraries and computer-resident databases are the tools that are most often used to satisfy the direct needs of intelligence analysts. These are often supplemented with exploitation of captured documents and personnel who are subjected to interrogation by skilled linguists trained and experienced in the art of asking questions. A famous example of the usefulness of captured enemy documents was the occasion in the American Civil War (1861–1865) on which a Confederate Army soldier was marching across Maryland during Robert E. Lee's invasion of Maryland (September 1862). This man absentmindedly lost three cigars wrapped in a piece of paper while taking a nap alongside the road during a break from marching. A Union Army soldier in the pursuing force found the cigars and, while smoking one, looked at the paper. It was a lost copy of General Lee's campaign order that gave the details of the locations of all the units of the Southern army for the next three days. General George McClellan, the Northern commander, did not really believe that this could be a genuine order and did not fully exploit the information. It is for this reason that he failed to soundly defeat Lee's forces at the Battle of Antietam (September 17, 1862), the single bloodiest day of battle of the entire Civil War; within a few weeks of that battle, he was removed from command of the Army of the Potomac.

Reconnaissance

Another crucial element of SIGINT is *reconnaissance*. This term essentially means scouting, or going on patrol to see where the enemy is located. Reconnaissance is generally thought to be a function of combat or military intelligence. Commanders often need to send troops either from general or "line" combat units or from specialized reconnaissance units to scout for the location of the enemy, to take prisoners for interrogation, or to "screen" (block) against enemy combat scouting. Rangers, Special Forces (Green Berets), and air or mechanized armored cavalry are all examples of units that are special "tools" for reconnaissance. In previous centuries, the cavalry performed most scouting of this kind.

During the Gettysburg Campaign in 1863, General Robert E. Lee sent most of his cavalry (around six thousand sabers) on an extended reconnaissance around the rear of the Union Army that was following him north as he invaded Pennsylvania from Virginia. The cavalry commander was Major General Jeb Stuart, one of the most colorful and romantic figures of the Civil War. His nickname from West Point days was "Beauty." He was a dashing cavalier and wherever he went young ladies turned out in numbers to see the famous horse soldier pass by. On this occasion, Stuart did not do his best work. He broke through into the enemy army's rear, but instead of maintaining contact with Lee's army so that he could pass information to his commander, Stuart rode into the deep rear of the Union Army, where he was of no use at all to Lee. He arrived at Gettysburg well after the great battle (July 1–3, 1863) had begun and played no major role in the fight. His failure to conduct effective reconnaissance is generally thought to be one of the major causes of the Confederate defeat at Gettysburg.

HUMINT

Human-Source Intelligence
Human-source intelligence, or HUMINT, is intelligence collected by means of agents or informers. This kind of collection includes

a number of different kinds of collectors. Some are open, or overt, and others are operators who recruit and use foreign personnel (and sometimes friendly personnel) to go within the enemy or potential enemy's position or country to spy and learn what they can of the deepest secrets.

Overt HUMINT

A great deal of information is available to those who go and ask for it openly. One such method is simple "debriefing." Commercial travelers, visiting scholars, and ordinary tourists all are excellent sources of information on foreign areas, especially areas in which there is no official representation by the country or military force seeking information on activity or personalities within that area. Often the method involves an interview by debriefing teams of linguists and specialists in the work of leading a source through a recounting of the story of his or her travels or residence. For decades during the Cold War, the NATO powers maintained debriefing centers in Germany, England, and various places in the United States. Travelers and others who had been to the territory of the Warsaw Pact or other sensitive areas were contacted and asked if they would agree to an interview. If they did, then they were "whisked away" to secret "safe sites," some of which were picturesque castles in the German mountains, for a government-sponsored vacation in which they had the ego-building experience of having someone spend hours asking questions about their ordinary activities. The resulting reports were often quite interesting. Many travelers in Eastern Europe saw things for which only serendipity could provide an explanation. Soviet troop movements, new weapons, and equipment in transit around the countryside were often observed. Reports on such things were commonplace.

Another mode of open collection of information is called "embassy diplomat open reporting." Every embassy on

Earth has a number of Foreign Service Officers assigned to it who have, as one of their most important jobs, reports that are to be sent to their country's foreign-affairs ministry at home in their own capital. Political officers, military attachés, economic officers, commercial officers—these are the typical jobs of the diplomatic staff in an embassy. These officers have a variety of functions; among these are to advise the ambassador (who is their boss) and to attend ceremonies of the host government or private groups to represent their country. But their most important job lies in writing reports that inform their government of the situation in the country in which they are stationed. In the course of their duties, such diplomatic officers attend a wide variety of host country meetings, conferences, and social events. Just by "being there," and by being good listeners and conversationalists, the embassy officers "pick up" a vast amount of good information. This open diplomatic reporting is immensely useful and is often the first "tip-off" that something important needs to be looked at more closely. In 1990, the Arab Middle East country of Iraq invaded its neighbor, Kuwait. The dictator of Iraq had long coveted Kuwait's oil wealth and had finally decided to conquer the country and take what he wanted. In pursuit of that goal, he began to mass the armored forces of his army next to Kuwait's border and to move his air force closer to Kuwait. To do that, he had to move masses of tanks, artillery guns, and troops from hundreds of miles deep inside Iraq south towards Kuwait over Iraq's excellent highways. This movement was easily detected by American satellite photography, and a telegraphic message went from Washington to the American Embassy in Baghdad asking that someone go out on the roads and verify the size and character of the troop movements taking place. The American military attaché went out immediately to do this, and his "on the scene" reporting was derived from standing by the side of the road. Watching what went by through trained eyes completed the Washington analysts' understanding of Iraq's preparations. Satellite photographs may provide "snapshots" taken from hundreds of miles in space; however, a good pair of eyes at ground level is always invaluable.

Clandestine HUMINT — Espionage (Spying)

"To historians, it is the world's second-oldest profession. To criminologists, it is a crime against the national governments that are the targets. To practitioners, it is the exercise of simple tradecraft."

Just about every country in the world uses spies to learn the secrets of the other "players" in the "game of nations." In general, this is done by those intelligence professionals of one country who are specialists in this work and who find citizens of the target country that have access to the desired information. They then determine what might induce the targeted person to give that information to the "friendly" agency even though the very act of giving is almost always illegal from the point of view of the agent's own country and usually will result in stern punishments, perhaps death, if uncovered. If the targeted person accepts the job of betraying his own country for the foreign intelligence agency, he is known "in the trade" as an "agent" or "asset." The intelligence professional is not an "agent." Only the foreign asset is called an agent. The intelligence professional is often called a "case officer" or an "agent handler." There are some police forces like the Federal Bureau of Investigation (FBI) who call their policemen "agents," or "special agents," but this terminology is never used in intelligence work where only the acquired "asset" can be called an "agent." This is an important distinction because agents are always thought to be expendable.

The business of clandestine collection of HUMINT always involves great risk of disclosure and political embarrassment, imprisonment, or even death for all concerned. Clandestine assets must be recruited and "handled" with great discretion and in secret. The problems involved in communicating with clandestine assets are immense and require great skill, as well as being very time and labor intensive. For these reasons and others, the case officers handling an operation are often "covered" (concealed) within an embassy or other government activity pretending to be something that they are not. Disclosure of their true work can lead to ruptures of diplomatic relations and other difficulties. For these reasons, governments try to limit the use of this kind of information collection to the most important "targets" in the smallest number of places possible. An estimate that clandestine collection amounts to 5 percent of the total collection effort is probably realistic. Nevertheless, the spy's trade is the indispensable 5 percent, because it is from the well-placed spy that one best learns with clarity what it is that the adversary has decided to do.

Unless an intelligence agency "gets lucky" in a major way, the more usual kinds of information collection mentioned above have one major defect. They do not usually reveal what the target's *intentions* might be. Satellite photography, library research, signals intelligence and all non-espionage means of information collection rarely yield direct indications of the enemy's intention. What they usually disclose is circumstantial evidence which, when taken together with all that is known of the situation, yields an *inferential* analytic conclusion based on *probability*. This often is good enough, but if the target is important enough, then only certain knowledge of the opponent's intention is acceptable as proof of future action.

Many intelligence services around the world have been given responsibilities by their government that have nothing to do with information gathering and analysis. Some have been given the task of conducting secret foreign policy activities for their governments. Some have been given propaganda activities as another mission. The main thing to remember is that, although these functions may reside in an intelligence agency, they are not properly intelligence and are always something of a distraction from the main business of information.

3

Arnold Deutsch:
A Master of
the Dark Art

"A source with access to the mind of the target."

It is normally only a human being with access to the mind of the adversary who can tell a government what the intention of the adversary is. Such a person is, in almost all cases, a member of the adversarial group, and for him to provide such information is usually treason or espionage under the local law. The famous case of Colonel Oleg Penkovsky of the GRU (Soviet Military Intelligence) is illustrative. As we discussed, Penkovsky volunteered his assistance to Western intelligence and provided the West with information that made Soviet *intentions* crystal clear. The "Red Orchestra" ring run by the GRU within the German Wehrmacht's World War II command structure is another such example.

Then there is Alger Hiss, who served his Communist "faith" and Soviet military intelligence as a senior official of the U.S. government for many years. It used to be a kind of "parlor game" for people in the United States to debate the issue of Hiss's guilt or innocence, with people taking positions over this topic that reflected their political inclinations. This discussion was effectively ended after the fall of the Soviet government in 1991, when access for scholars to the files of the Soviet government conclusively proved Hiss's guilt. At about the same time, the release to the public of the decrypted "Venona" telegrams added nails to Hiss's coffin. Penalties were (and still are) severe for those apprehended. Hiss was convicted of perjury in testimony concerning his membership in the Communist Party, and his long career as a "public man" was destroyed forever.

The art of recruiting, handling, and controlling such people in the interests of one's own country is called "clandestine collection" of human intelligence (HUMINT). HUMINT denotes all sorts of collection through the agency of human sources. Some of them are not at all hidden and in fact are quite open; these have already been mentioned. It can be understood from this that all clandestine collection is HUMINT, but not all HUMINT is clandestine.

The clandestine services of a country are defined as "those elements of the intelligence community of a state that are specialized in the use of human assets (agents) to collect information of high value in foreign countries where such collection is illegal under local law." It is sometimes the case that governments group together in the same "apparatus" the clandestine collection force and other entities that carry out the necessarily secret will of a state. These activities include covert paramilitary action, secret police units, black propaganda, secret interventions in the political life of an adversary, and *disinformatsiya*, or disinformation, an art perfected by the Soviets that still is named by a Russian word. To group together some or all of these functions with clandestine collection of information is a common practice beloved by resource managers, but it is a fundamental mistake. This is because the skills, knowledge base, and very personality traits needed by the clandestine recruiter and handler are quite different from those needed in these other specialties. To put all these functions together in one organization is to risk distortion of the clandestine collection function by those who do not understand it or even appreciate it.

Why would this be the case? Why would direction of clandestine collection by someone from the police, commandos, or resource management be destructive of this function? The answer is in the nature of the work itself. The success of all these other fields of effort either depend on the use of the power of the state in some way to intimidate, coerce or direct cooperation and acquiescence or they similarly employ "trickery" of some kind to achieve the same "ends." These "ends" are the goal of assisting the state in creating a new, different, and hopefully more favorable future. In other words, they are in the business of policy implementation.

On the other hand, clandestine collection, like all the true intelligence functions, seeks not to *create* reality but to *describe* it—to find human resources who have the necessary access to key information, and to *persuade* these people to risk everything to give this information to the clandestine operator and to give it willingly, honestly, and reliably. How is such persuasion possible? There are clandestine services or individuals within them who have relied upon bribery, blackmail, or the provision of sexual services to agents in order to recruit and control. There are cases in which this has worked well, sometimes for extended periods of time. Examples come to mind: Aldrich Ames of the CIA spied for the KGB for money alone, as did the spies run by the Soviets within the U.S. Navy (Whittaker and Walker). The Soviet services were infamous for their use of "swallows" (females used to seduce and control foreign "assets"). Nevertheless, such relationships between a clandestine operator and a source are inherently unstable and unreliable because they do not engage the loyalty of the source. Sources who have been recruited or controlled through such methods are much given to fabricating information, to "marketing" information to several services, or are likely to fail in pursuit of really valuable information because they will not take risks.

The truly great "coups" scored by clandestine collection over the centuries have been the result of the ability of gifted clandestine operators to recognize the needs—not the vulnerabilities—of potential sources of the needed information, and to convince those sources that the clandestine officer is the key to fulfilling those needs. It is not necessary that the potential source's notion that the clandestine operator holds the key to fulfillment be *correct*. In fact, in most cases it is not; but it is essential that the source believe without hesitation that his or her wants can be met by the clandestine service (or whatever it is that the clandestine service portrays itself to be). Actually, it is seldom possible that a government agency that is engaged in the work of a state can really be, or wish to be, the road to "salvation" for *anyone*. Government agencies are goal-oriented and properly focused on the information requirements of policy. They are essentially uninterested in the trauma, spiritual hunger, political desire, and deprivation that make people susceptible to recruitment for espionage work. This creates a certain problem, for it is precisely these features of injured personality that make one person reach out to another for solace. Therefore, it is the role of the clandestine operator to stand between the cold reality of his service's essential disinterest in the human needs of its sources and the sources' *need* to believe otherwise—that, in fact, the service will value and care for them.

What sort of person can successfully fulfill such a role? Typically, it is someone who projects a deep and abundant empathy; someone who is the quintessential "listener," someone whom the source believes really does care about him, someone in whom the source finds the comfort missing from the rest of his or her life. At the same time, the clandestine operator must bifurcate himself internally so that, while he is one person to the source, he is someone altogether different to his own service. For his own organization he must be a calculating manipulator of human beings, a dedicated public servant who places the tasks assigned by his country's leaders above sentiment and who is prepared to sacrifice his sources for the greater good at any time. Such people do not "grow on trees." They are the product both of a certain predisposition and a long course of preparation in both education and training.

An example of the level of performance that can be reached by someone in whom training and education come together with experience (the best kind of training) is the case of Arnold Deutsch. He was born into the world of Central European Jewry in the last decade of the nineteenth century, and early in life he became a socialist. With the establishment of Bolshevik rule in Russia in 1917, he easily became a member of the Communist Party, serving first in the Comintern apparatus and later in the NKVD itself as a career officer. In his pre-party life as a son of the bourgeoisie in middle Europe, Deutsch studied at several first-rate universities. An enormously intelligent man, he became so learned in the humanities that in France he would easily have been included among the elite ranks of the *aggrégés*. As a dedicated Chekist, he acquired a vast experience of "conspiratorial work," as his comrades would have called it. His talent for the work led to his assignment in the mid-1930s to the NKVD station in London, where he was "covered" as a minor embassy official. In London, he found a scope for his talents that exceeded reasonable expectation. Britain was locked in the deep despair that gripped it in the aftermath of World War I; its most promising sons had been "wasted" in Flanders, Mesopotamia, and a hundred other places. Their younger brothers inhabited the privileged world of "Oxbridge"—the prestigious British universities of Oxford and Cambridge—and immersed themselves in well-bred angst over the supposed "failure" of old values and faiths. A great many of them flirted with socialism, communism, and other pseudo-religious belief systems of the left. In this, they were mightily encouraged by a number of faculty members. These same faculty members reported the presence of their most "promising" students, especially those who had little visible connection with the left. This information was passed through the British Communist Party (BCP) to the embassy in London, where Deutsch and his

Mata Hari: Accidental spy? The name Mata Hari ("Eye of Dawn") is synonymous with espionage—but it is unclear just how much of a spy she was. By World War I, she was famous throughout Europe as an exotic dancer and a courtesan and had lovers on both sides of the French-German border. She is known to have worked for the French Secret Service for a time and may have traded sensitive information among her paramours. The French, the Germans, and the British all suspected her.

Early in 1917, she was arrested in France and blamed for the deaths of thousands of soldiers. She was convicted at a closed trial, on thin evidence, and executed by firing squad later that year. Her guilt was never conclusively proven, though, and the French files on Mata Hari remain sealed to this day.

WARNING

from the

FBI

The war against spies and saboteurs demands the aid of every American.

When you see evidence of sabotage, notify the Federal Bureau of Investigation at once.

When you suspect the presence of enemy agents, tell it to the FBI.

Beware of those who spread enemy propaganda! Don't repeat vicious rumors or vicious whispers.

Tell it to the FBI!

J. Edgar Hoover, *Director*
Federal Bureau of Investigation

The nearest Federal Bureau of Investigation office is listed on page one of your telephone directory.

Warning from the FBI. This is one of many posters created during World War II by the Office of War Information, which handled the propaganda surrounding the war. Similar posters warned that careless talk could endanger American soldiers or urged Americans to buy war bonds or conserve or sacrifice supplies.

The poster was signed by J. Edgar Hoover, who directed the FBI between 1924 and his death in 1972. Hoover believed there were Communist spies throughout the federal government. He investigated every suspect, and the information he obtained gave him power over thousands of public figures. The notorious House Un-American Activities Committee depended on him; Hoover leaked information about Alger Hiss and made it possible to convict the Rosenbergs. He later investigated civil rights leaders and opponents of the Vietnam War. Most of his extensive private files, which held thousands in fear, were destroyed when he died.

The Pumpkin Papers. The espionage trial of Alger Hiss in 1949 was a scandal. Hiss was a Harvard-educated lawyer who represented the United States at the Yalta Conference in 1945. Journalist Whittaker Chambers, a "reformed" spy for the Soviets who now was turning in his accomplices, accused Hiss of working with him. Hiss denied knowing Chambers but equivocated on several points; an investigation of Hiss followed but was inconclusive. Hiss sued Chambers for the accusations, and in response Chambers produced microfilmed documents, including this one, that he claimed proved Hiss's complicity. Afraid that the documents would fall into Hiss's hands and be destroyed, Chambers had hidden them in a hollowed-out pumpkin.

The statute of limitations on espionage had expired, so Hiss was convicted of perjury. His involvement was never proven, but the "Venona" documents, released by the U.S. government in 1996, do mention a Soviet spy in the American delegation to Yalta.

The Rosenbergs. The story of Julius and Ethel Rosenberg illustrates the anti-Communist hysteria of the early 1950s. In 1944, while working on the Manhattan Project at Los Alamos, Ethel's brother David Greenglass had sent some schematics to the Soviets through his wife, Ruth. He was investigated, and in exchange for a light sentence and immunity for his wife he agreed to implicate the Rosenbergs. At the Rosenberg trial, Ruth testified that Julius had been her link to the KGB, that Ethel had typed David's notes about the bomb, and that the Rosenbergs, avowed Communists, had masterminded the whole operation. All four were convicted; David went to prison for fifteen years, and Ruth served no time. The Rosenbergs, after imprisonment and some behind-the-scenes politics, were executed in June 1953. They protested their innocence to the end. Later investigations implicated Julius clearly, but David Greenglass eventually said that he had lied about Ethel's involvement.

Gary Powers before the Senate. In 1950, the CIA commissioned the U-2 spy plane as a means of conducting surveillance of the USSR; the plane was to fly at altitudes high enough to be undetectable by Soviet radar. Francis Gary Powers, a pilot with the Air Force, joined the U-2 program in 1956, just as flights over Soviet territory began. Four years later, on May 1, 1960, Soviet forces shot down his plane near Yekaterinburg (Sverdlovsk), in the central USSR. In accordance with U.S. policy of the time, officials claimed the flight had been gathering meteorological information. The Soviets, who had found surveillance equipment on the plane, angrily rejected this explanation and tried Powers for espionage. He was convicted and sentenced to seven years in prison. The United States exchanged him for a captured Soviet spy in 1962, and this photograph was taken as Powers was debriefed by the Senate Armed Forces Committee.

Kim Philby of the Cambridge Spies. Arnold Deutsch recruited the men who would later be known as the Cambridge Spies in the 1930s, while they were still college students. Speaking publicly against communism, they went on to important positions in the British government; they then used their access to leak sensitive information to the USSR. Two of them, Guy Burgess and Donald Maclean, defected to the Soviet Union in 1951, and Harold "Kim" Philby (shown here at right) followed in 1963. Anthony Blunt, who held both a knighthood and a royal commission, and John Cairncross both confessed in the 1960s in exchange for immunity. Philby was among the most successful of the group; after his "retirement," he lived like a hero in Moscow. Despite the two confessions, many questions concerning the activities of the Cambridge Spies were never resolved.

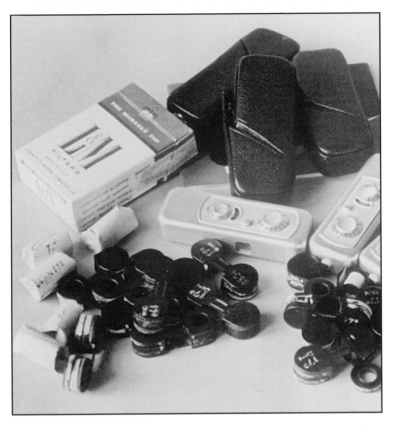

Evidence in the Penkovsky trial. Oleg Penkovsky, a Russian scientific worker and war hero, was one of the United States' most important assets in the Soviet Union during the Cold War. Penkovsky disagreed with the policies of Nikita Khrushchev's government (1953–1964), so he gave information on Soviet military capabilities to both the United States and the United Kingdom.

Penkovsky was eventually discovered, and the Soviets tried him in Moscow in May of 1963. He pleaded guilty, but Soviet authorities offered these mini-cameras and microfilms, along with a cigarette packet used to hide the films, as espionage equipment they had seized from him. Penkovsky was convicted and shot for treason. Nevertheless, the Penkovsky relationship, which ran through the Eisenhower and Kennedy administrations, was probably the era's most successful espionage operation.

The Walker spy ring. The spy ring led by John A. Walker, Jr., is among the most notorious in the history of American espionage. As a high-ranking officer in the navy, Walker had access to classified encryption techniques. In 1968, he began to sell navy secrets to the Soviets through their embassy in Washington. He later recruited his son, his brother, and a friend, all of whom had access to classified military information.

Walker's ex-wife finally reported him to the FBI in 1984. The FBI investigated, and Walker and his coconspirators were arrested early in 1985. This photograph was taken in October of that year, as Walker (left) was escorted by a U.S. marshal to federal court in Baltimore. All four members of the Walker spy ring—who had compromised a million navy communications and endangered thousands of lives—were convicted and sentenced to decades in prison.

fellow Chekists contemplated it. Deutsch, who was not *Rezident* (chief) of the NKVD station, conceived the idea that what should be done was to recruit a number of the more interesting students at the two universities as long-term "investments" who could then be encouraged to enter various aspects of British life in the "Establishment" at some time in the future. His boss, the Rezident, accepted this plan and gave his blessing to Deutsch's project. Deutsch was then placed in contact with the students through "casual" meetings arranged by the British Communist Party working through the professors. From this arrangement emerged the infamous ring of Soviet spies known as the "Cambridge Five"—or is it Six, or maybe Seven?—Guy Burgess, Donald Maclean, Harold "Kim" Philby, Anthony Blunt, John Cairncross, and others.

The exact details of what happened next at Oxford are unknown but can easily be guessed and are discussed below. In any event, Deutsch recruited them all and trained them thoroughly. Then, at Deutsch's instruction, this group of agents broke off any contact that they had with the left, and in some cases, became vocal anticommunists. They graduated and went out into the world "programmed" to succeed in British public life, and with the possible exception of Guy Burgess, they did succeed. Maclean and Cairncross rose in the British Foreign Office; Philby was always a success, first as a journalist, then as a very senior officer of MI-6, (the British version of the American CIA). Blunt was, for many years, a senior official in MI-5 (British counter-intelligence). He also inhabited the very heart of the art establishment as Curator of the Queen's Pictures. Burgess's drunkenness and homosexual indiscretions kept him from realizing his considerable potential.

Once these "children" were his, Deutsch had a fairly short time with them. The year was 1936, and Stalin's madness and tyrannical suspicion were directed at everyone around him, and especially at "Old Bolsheviks," intelligence men, and Jewish people. Deutsch fit nicely into all three categories, as did most of his colleagues in London and across the world. One by one they were recalled to Moscow Center for "consultations" from which they rarely returned. The men from the London station *never* returned—*none* of them, not one. Stalin was particularly keen to eliminate them as a group. He believed that what they claimed to have accomplished, as a group, in recruiting these university students could not be real. Deutsch had been the principal actor in this case, but everyone in the station had participated and the Rezident insisted that these were not only well recruited agents, but devoted Communists as well. To Stalin, this insistence only proved that either the NKVD men in London were so naive as to be criminally negligent or they were attempting to "sell" this fairy tale to him on behalf of British intelligence. Either way, they had to die—and die they did. Arnold Deutsch was killed in one of the tiled basement execution rooms of the Lubyanka Prison in Moscow. His reward for creating an entirely new doctrine of operations for Soviet intelligence was a small-caliber bullet to the back of the head.

For Deutsch's "children," it was a puzzling time. Not only were they concerned about the rumors they heard of events in Russia, but, also, gradually their contact with the station in

Joseph Stalin and Espionage

Joseph Stalin shares with Adolf Hitler the "honor" (and shame) of having been the most feared and cruel dictator of the twentieth century. Stalin became the absolute ruler of the Union of Soviet Socialist Republics (USSR) upon the death of Vladimir Lenin, who founded the USSR in the early 1920s. By an odd irony of history, Stalin had first become associated with the Bolshevik Communist underground through his work as a secret informer for the tsar's secret police, the *Okhrana*. Stalin infiltrated the Bolsheviks for the tsar so thoroughly that he became Lenin's most trusted lieutenant and eventually his successor. Once in power, Stalin used the Soviet intelligence service (the NKVD) with great ruthlessness to penetrate Western governments and societies, employing local Communist parties as recruiting screeners.

London dried up and ended as one by one the NKVD men were recalled and killed. Finally, they were completely alone, without contacts in their organization, isolated by the discipline of clandestine communications that Deutsch had taught them. They knew that the British watched the embassy and that to blindly seek to contact the Soviets at the embassy would probably destroy them. Therefore, they "went to ground"— hid—and waited, and waited, and waited. After nearly two years, someone new arrived, someone who knew their "recognition signal," someone to bring them back to life. This representative of the newly reopened London station was astonished. For two years these fledgling agents had kept themselves ready, had trained one another, had spotted and assessed more prospects for recruitment, and, most important from the Communist point of view, had continued their "political education" in secret seminars held in their rooms. Deutsch's dead hand had guided them. They were his children still, and they had not failed him. How is it that Deutsch established such complete dominance over the minds of these brilliant young men? What was it about him or what he did that gave him the key to their souls? If we know that, we may know what it is that an "ace" clandestine operator must be.

As a professor, Deutsch discovered people who were the most likely "candidates." From these "spotters" he also knew much about the personalities, background, and state of education of each of the "possibles." He knew what each person thought he wanted in life. He knew of the men's hunger for justice in the world. He knew how to talk to each one. What followed must have been easy for him. He met them, singly and in groups in a hundred pubs, restaurants, picnics, concert halls, and dormitory "bull sessions." He spent a lot of time sitting on park benches talking to them and smoking the "evil" old briar pipe that Philby would remember for the rest of his life. There he was, a "tweedy" young tutor with a charming Central European accent, erudite and persuasive, all that he should be—

and all that *they* should be. He came to represent to them their better selves, their hope for worthwhile lives. He did not recruit them; they recruited themselves. In the end, they *asked* to be "taken in," like strays seeking a home. And like strays, they were forever loyal to their new master and benefactor.

A well-run clandestine operation does not seek to "turn" unmotivated humans and cause them to become agents of a foreign power engaged in espionage. Instead, it searches among those who have access or who can come to have access for those special people who have hungers and needs that can be used in controlling them. Once the presence and nature of such needs are established, then a suitable operative is employed to make contact and begin the "development" of the source. In this development, the operative gradually "reveals" to the source the evidence that "proves" that the operative is the answer to the source's problem. As has been stated before, this "proof" may be entirely spurious—or it may be quite genuine, as in Deutsch's case. It may even be that the operative has portrayed himself to be something or someone other than he really is, perhaps even a representative of something other than his own country. The "hungers" of prospective sources are as varied as human nature. There are the more noble hungers, such as those for national independence, liberty, justice, ideology, or environmental improvement; and there are the more ignoble hungers, fed by egotism, spite, vengefulness, or envy. The nature of the hunger is unimportant to the clandestine collection team. It is the strength of the hunger that matters, as well as the clarity of the source's identification of the fulfillment of his need in the operative.

It can be seen from this discussion that the operative and the source are "locked" together in a symbiotic relationship. The source needs the operative both emotionally and often materially, and the operative needs the source to satisfy his mission and his superiors. It is a tragedy of this kind of work that in order to recruit and "run" agents against significant targets one must exploit sources who are "substantial" people,

people of some intellect and/or sophistication. Operatives who can do this must become very close to the source, so close that they are often suspected of "falling in love" with the source. Romance is not implied here, but a lack of objectivity certainly is. This tendency is a constant danger. The more sophisticated the sources, and the more empathic and effective the operative, the greater the danger. In thinking of this, it is necessary to remember that, except in rare cases, the source is not a member of the clandestine service, is a foreign national, and is generally thought to be expendable by the sponsoring government if that becomes necessary for *raisons d'état* (reasons of state).

The Recruiter

There are some skills and disciplines that, like fine art, are truly timeless and ageless: medicine, philosophy, poetry, and espionage. Some human activities are universally "portable." Is "recruiting" for espionage one of them, based in the universality of humanity's basic need for knowledge and desire for acceptance and spiritual solace? Or is it specific to a time and place, a product of a particular culture's inability to cope with the unhappiness of some of its members and the opportunistic readiness of another culture to take advantage of this? Perhaps it is both.

This is a subject worth thinking about, for recruiting is a skill that lies at the heart of espionage. Some operatives are more or less born with this talent, and some learn it. Others are condemned to it by their character.

Some of the tactics and principles of recruiting are best learned through direct experience, but narration provides a convenient substitute. With this in mind, consider the following passage from *The Butcher's Cleaver*, the author's novel of Confederate espionage and Union counterintelligence in the American Civil War.

The story concerns a Confederate infantry captain named Claude Devereux, a cultured, well-traveled, and educated man of wealth and high social position who was a banker in Alexandria, Virginia, before the breakup of the federal Union in 1861. Devereux has been chosen by his government to infiltrate Union Army–occupied northern Virginia, return to his hometown, and build a Southern espionage "ring" in Washington, D.C.; his larger mission is to penetrate the inner circles of the Lincoln administration to learn its weaknesses. Devereux is an unhappy man who has searched all his life for the friendship of some "band of brothers" who would accept him for what he is by nature—a brilliant but eccentric and skeptical personality. He has found this camaraderie in his combat unit, of which he is a respected and valued member. Against his wishes, he has been directed to leave his unit to take up the difficult and unrewarding task of "living a lie" among his enemies. In the past winter, that of 1861–1862, Devereux spent a month among his family and friends in Alexandria, studying the feasibility of such a project. From his point of view, this mission was a disaster, because his success has caused the Confederacy to send him back, this time permanently. He does not want this task.

In the late winter of 1862–1863, Devereux is in Ashland, Virginia, a town just north of the Confederate capital of Richmond and situated along the tracks of the Richmond,

General Samuel Cooper and the Signal Corps

In the Army of the Confederate States of America (CSA), the intelligence function was subordinated to the Adjutant General of the Confederate Army (TAG). Throughout the war, this was General Samuel Cooper. Cooper had been the Adjutant General of the U.S. Army before the war and had written extensively on staff functions. He exercised control over the Confederate War Department Secret Service through the organization known in that army as the Signal Corps. This branch of the army had little to do with communication and everything to do with spying and covert sabotage operations in the North. The Signal Corps operated a secret line of transportation across the Potomac River south of Washington and transported agents back and forth across the river throughout the war.

Fredericksburg, and Potomac Railroad. Throughout the Civil War, the Southern government maintained a center of training and operations control at a hotel in Ashland. This site was used for the instruction of agents and for the briefing and debriefing of those dispatched into the North.

Over the course of the Civil War, several European countries played with the idea of intervening in order to force the United States to accept the independence of the Confederacy; the most likely mode of intervention would have been to break the Union naval blockade of the South. The interest of the Europeans in this possibility was strongest in the first two years of the war, when it still seemed likely that the South was strong enough to defeat the North. Later in the war, when the South was losing, the Europeans lost interest in providing the help that would have been needed for the South to become a separate country. If that seems cynical on the Europeans' part, it should be remembered that, in a truism ascribed to various leaders of international politics, "countries do not have friends; they only have interests." Cynicism, or realism, as some would insist, is a common feature in international relations. Such an attitude is also found in the business world, where it is notoriously true that banks are interested in lending money only where it is not deeply needed.

It has long been a matter of oral tradition in the South that the British government surreptitiously helped the Confederacy in several ways in the early days of "the War." It is believed that among those "helps" was a training and advisory mission that assisted the South in creating a secret service. The locus of this assistance has long been believed to be the little hotel at Ashland, Virginia (which now is one of the central edifices of Randolph-Macon College).

In the following passage, Captain Claude Devereux of the 17th Virginia Infantry is introduced to the two Englishmen posing in America as immigrants to the South. These men have been given a limited exposure to him and his operational assistant, Bill White, in order to impart to them the essence of the clandestine operator's art.

At two o'clock they began. The two Englishmen had spent a great deal of time in the solarium. You could see it in the comfortable sprawl of the huge one and the automatic reach with which the small, rabbity one placed his teacup almost exactly on the stain in the wooden tabletop. . . . They claimed to be recent immigrants, newly embarked on patriotic volunteer work for "the cause." The big, fat one was named Philip Hare, and the little one wished to be known as Henry Rocklin. The fat man beamed at Devereux.

"Understand you speak French. Lovely language, lovely folk, lovely women!" He began a rambling discourse on the marvels of Gallic civilization in a French that Devereux heard with growing amusement. It was perfectly fluent, but it appeared to have been learned on the Marseilles docks. Claude smiled at the thought of the embarrassment that his mother would experience to hear the vulgarity of some of the idioms.

White was in his seat in the corner, just behind Devereux. . . . Bill thought himself a good judge of people. This fat man's jocularity and good humor were not genuine. The little man was very odd. One eye was larger than the other. His clothing looked expensive but inappropriate. A linen suit was too light for the season.

They said they had served together in the Indian Police, gradually working their way over the years into the management of confidential informants as a trade.

Devereux was a good listener. Voices had special meaning for him. The two were upper-class in their diction. British men of their origins did not serve in the colonial police. The little one had something of the British army officer about him. Devereux shared the prejudice of many Americans of his time against the British. The possibility of their support against the United States might make cooperation necessary, but the memory of parliamentary oppression and two wars was yet strong. Nevertheless, he rose to the occasion and remarked that it was certainly fortunate for the South that they were available to help with their experience in these things.

Rocklin rubbed his too-large eye. "Colonel—it is 'colonel,' I believe?"

Claude thought about this. How intriguing—these foreigners are clearly establishment types. They have been given a less-than-complete knowledge of his task by Jenkins. This must mean that these two wanderers are with us, but not of us. Jenkins must believe that these two would restrict their conversation to that which was immediately at hand. How surprisingly naïve! How unlike him. . . . "Yes, lieutenant colonel, in fact," he said.

The rabbit beamed, delighted to know that he might get more from this talk than a chance to impart his hard-won skills. "We are informed that your mission will take you into the capital city," he said.

"You mean Washington City?" Claude replied evenly.

The rabbit smiled again, but the teeth looked bigger this time. "Quite so, quite so, not Richmond. It is likely that you will find it advantageous to get the private assistance of persons who already have the information that is wanted."

Claude did not disagree.

"Tell me, Colonel, how do you think one does this?" the rabbit asked.

After some thought, Claude began, "I imagine that it would be profitable to think of this as a form of seduction. The desired person is cultivated, flattered, fêted. Attention is showered. Identification is sought between the goal and that which the intended victim thinks he or she wishes to do. At some point a gradual acquiescence and action are obtained." He stopped.

Hare looked out at the lawn. Rocklin grinned. "You have done this before."

Claude thought of the circle he had built in Alexandria the previous winter. He thought of his friends and the necessity of protecting them from these men. "No, not in this work," he lied, "but I have the usual knowledge of seduction and the process must be a lot like tying up a bargain in international commerce. *That* I know a lot about."

The big man stopped smiling and nodding at the lawn. Hare turned to focus on Devereux looking unconvinced. "Colonel, most of what you say is correct, but you have failed to describe the most difficult step." The big, square head continued to speak. . . . "We have found that only by rare chance and in odd circumstance is it possible to 'seduce' someone who does not wish it." Seeing that he had Devereux's undivided attention, he went on. "What must be done is to make an appreciation of the approximate locale in which the right man or woman might be found, and then one must spread wide the net."

"And," Rocklin added, "one listens, and looks and feels, waiting for the moment when a sensitive soul discovers in another, a secret hunger which must be satisfied."

"Does it matter what the hunger craves?" Devereux was whispering now. There was something about this discussion that was darkly disquieting.

The big head spoke. "Very little, actually. As a general thing, almost any hunger is of use. It matters not how praiseworthy or despicable that hunger might be."

Rocklin recommenced. "One dreams, of course, of discovering a cabinet minister who harbors an overpowering desire to associate himself with one's cause from political conviction, but alas, a desire for vengeance or simple lust is more common."

"And after this hungering soul is discovered and diagnosed, I should apply my ideas of seduction?" Devereux found this line of talk deeply absorbing. Something in it gripped his mind, forbidding the indulgence in other paths of thought so common to him in talks like this. For some reason he suddenly thought of his grandfather as he looked in dreams.

The rabbit grew enthusiastic. "Gradually, gradually, being careful not to frighten the quarry. Slowly you must associate the hunger with your task in the mind of the victim, slowly becoming more demanding in return for your apparent efforts to slake the need."

With shattering suddenness, Devereux knew he was hearing his own vulnerability described. *If this is how it is done, who better than me to do it?* he thought. He eyed the smaller man. "I didn't know they had cabinet ministers in India," he said.

The big one rumbled, deep in the chest. "Well done! After your return I reckon we'll have a good idea of the strength of Hooker's army?"

The pathetic obviousness of the attempt to fish for the details of his task aroused his contempt. "Perhaps so," Devereux replied. "I intend to look around in the British embassy for possible friends. Do you know anyone there?"

The bait lay on the table; nearly visible. . . . It was so touchingly evident.

The little fellow spoke: "Not really. The only man we know there is the assistant military attaché, Major Neville. He might be someone to discuss things with, if the chance arose."

Surely Jenkins must know this! Devereux thought. *He must know these Limey bastards are playing their own game.* "I'll remember," he said.

"Why don't we stop for tea?" Hare asked pleasantly. "You and your chap take a stroll in this lovely park and then come back. We want to talk to you about hidden communication with informants and ways to deal with the police if they are pesky."

5

The Operational Cycle: Targeting, Development, and Recruitment

MISSION ASSIGNMENT AND ANALYSIS

Espionage organizations are always part of a larger whole. Usually, they are embedded in the structure of a national intelligence agency or in the military intelligence apparatus that supports an army, air force, or navy in active military operations or in the perennial international struggles among governments to achieve a meaningful advantage in weaponry.

In most circumstances the intelligence assets of a state are tasked for collection work by something called "The National Council for Security" or some similar name. In the usual structure of government, this body is made up of the head of government, the ministers of defense and foreign relations, and the chiefs of staff of the armed forces of the country. Such a body establishes priorities for collection efforts by the country's available assets (diplomats, intelligence agencies, and the armed forces of a country at the national level). These priorities are translated into documents that are sent to affected government groups for action.

In the case of military forces involved in combat operations or expecting to enter combat operations, the commander of the military force involved has a group of officers around him, a staff, among whose tasks is providing the commander with the information he needs to make a variety of essential decisions about operations, logistics (supply, personnel, etc.), and intelligence. This staff's function in the job of deciding what information should be collected to support operational planning is no different from that of a "National Council for Security" staff, except that the information that it will be seeking for the commander is more specifically military in nature and has to do with targets, enemy strengths and positions, morale, state of supply, obstacles, and many other related matters. The commander makes his choices about the information he most wants based on his staff's recommendation. These priority requests, which are referred to as Essential Elements of Information, or EEI, move through the hierarchy in three ways: upward to the national intelligence community; downward to military units subordinate to the planning headquarters; and also to specialized centers of intelligence analysis that belong to the armed forces.

Of all these tasks, only a very few are properly sent to the espionage activities of a government or army. Why is this? Basically, it is because espionage operations are inherently difficult, extremely dangerous, and, in the case of State Against State operations, likely to lead to major problems in international relations if they are uncovered and publicized. Therefore, it is a nearly universal truth in intelligence activities that espionage is used to gather information only when key technical or diplomatic documents must be obtained or when conclusive evidence of the target's intention is the only thing that will do.

TARGETING THE INFORMATION

Based on the tasking received, a clandestine intelligence activity seeks to identify the most effective "path" to reach the information that it is directed to get. It is very rarely possible to use a member of the clandestine service to obtain the needed documents or information *directly*. Because this information is important to the target country, it is carefully guarded and kept as secrets surrounded by layer after layer of security precautions. Among these precautions is always a careful exclusion of anyone whose loyalty is in doubt. In practice, these measures mean that foreigners, as well as anyone of doubtful provenance, are excluded from the information sources. Because of this security, it is usually necessary to find a member of the foreign government or armed forces who is willing to "betray his own" and provide what is needed. This reality reduces the search for a source to an analysis of where to look and among what group of possible recruits to handle such a desperate and dangerous job. It is natural to think that the best place to look for such a person is among high-ranking officials or military officers who need to work with the material and thus have easy access to it. Sometimes this has proven to be a good and sound way to search for a prospective source. The case of the Soviet colonel Oleg Penkovsky, which was mentioned earlier, is a perfect example of this. This is also true of Alger Hiss, who was a high official of the American government for many years and who provided very valuable information to Soviet military intelligence for a long time. The problem with targeting such senior personnel is that, by virtue of their very seniority, the target country's security organizations watch them more closely— their everyday actions are more easily noticed because of their prominence. This presents a myriad of difficulties in communicating with them once they are "recruited." In addition to this obstacle, there is also an inherent difficulty in having enough access to such senior people over a period of time long enough to make a recruitment.

Often senior officials are recruited simply because they "volunteer," as Penkovsky did. This is called a "walk-in" in the espionage trade and is more common a phenomenon than one might think. Hiss was a dedicated long-term member of the "underground" section of the American Communist Party that infiltrated the U.S. government as a matter of party discipline; in other words, he was obeying orders from his Communist superiors. In many such cases, the biggest problem is that the "walk-in" may present himself to a friendly government official who lacks the imagination or initiative to be receptive.

Because of the many barriers to the "recruitment" of senior personnel, this is seldom attempted. Instead, a search is made for target-country junior personnel who also have the required access to the desired information. Clerks, drivers (who overhear a lot), servants, guards, and couriers all are likely targets. Access to such people is much easier for the espionage service. They are often in more difficult economic circumstances and in need of money. They are often less committed to the "cause" of the target entity. Some of them harbor resentments over real or imagined social slights from their own people because of their low rank. They may also have what is sometimes called "the Iago complex"; Iago in Shakespeare's *Othello* at first seems to hate his boss just because he is the boss. Altogether, junior members of the target organization are an "easier mark" than are members of higher rank.

A good example of the use of such an agent is the celebrated case of Elyeza Bazna, whose code name was "Cicero." During World War II, Bazna served as personal valet to the British ambassador to Turkey. From the vantage point of his employment in the ambassador's household he was able to inform his German masters of the contents of the telegrams the ambassador received daily, as well as the details of the diplomatic discussions between Turkey and Britain about a possible British-German alliance. (A novel based on this story was filmed as *5 Fingers* in 1952, with James Mason in the role of "Cicero.")

SPOTTING AND ASSESSING PROSPECTIVE SOURCES

Once the collection "outfit" has analyzed the target and decided on what sort of population to focus its recruiting efforts, the process of identifying *particular* prospects begins. In this process, it is necessary, as Philip Hare says to Claude Devereux in *The Butcher's Cleaver*, to "cast a wide net." Whole categories of people, such as clerks or communication technicians, must be considered with all the information available to narrow the field of prospects to a number that is manageable for the limited personnel of the collection unit. Newspaper and Internet searches for evidence of access to the target are useful, as are many other kinds of openly available "library" kinds of information. In some cases, several sources of information will begin to create a kind of matrix of indicators that point to a particular person; further research may then disclose vulnerabilities or needs that indicate that this person may be approachable in ways that at least seem to be plausibly appealing to the source. In other cases, such as those of the "Cambridge Sleepers" recruited by Arnold Deutsch, cooperating "civilians" or "friends" of the collection service "spot" promising candidates for recruitment. They typically do this because of ideological affinity with the cause represented by the collection service. In this phase of the operation, all possible efforts are made to know all that can be known of the prospective agent, so that when this person is approached by the service it will be on the basis of "shared" interests leading to a "revelation" that the candidate source and the developing service have much in common.

DEVELOPMENT

If possible, as many different candidate agents are identified as time allows. Based on these identifications, an effort is mounted to obtain direct access to this person. Sometimes this is not possible and it is necessary to use an intermediary who can make an introduction. This intermediary may be a previously recruited agent or simply a friendly "bystander" who wants to help. In some cases, a process known as "daisy chaining" is employed, in which a string of contacts is used first to make an introduction and then to pass the prospective source from one friendly contact to another until direct access of the collection agency to the potential recruit is established. A primary reason for doing this is to keep the potential source, who will eventually be asked to spy for the collection service, from associating that "pitch" in his mind with the already recruited agent(s) who made the initial introduction. This is important to protect the identity and security of a valuable asset of the service from both (1) identification by someone who may become another asset of that service, and (2) the danger that might result from the failure of a recruitment attempt involving the potential source.

The goal in this process is to bring a case officer of the collection service into more or less continual contact with the potential source in order that, through a personal relationship, the case officer can assess the usefulness, stability, susceptibility to discipline, and real access of the potential source. Once the collection agency case officer has established this kind of contact, an assessment must be made of what would be the best appeal to make to this source to accept the tremendous risks in spying against those who think he is still "one of them." In some cases a potential source may seem unwilling to "work" for the collection service because he does not want to be associated in his mind with the collection service's sponsoring country. This may be a personal matter for him or her. In such cases, the collection service may well "make believe" and portray itself as representing some political or other entity than the sponsoring country. This tactic is called "false flagging."

What kinds of approach are possible? There are many, and some of them can be used together because they reinforce one another. Some approaches include patriotism; a hatred of a regime, especially an oppressive one; and the dislike of one ethnic or religious group or another. This is especially true if another group, one to whom the prospective agent is not sympathetic, rules the agent's own ethnic group. Money, too, is often a major factor in making a recruitment. This is as much true from the point of view of the collection service as it is from the vantage point of the "recruit." The reason is that, while the prospective agent may or may not want or need the money, the service needs the agent to take material rewards from it to establish a kind of "employer-employee" relationship; this helps to establish the service's positive control over the actions of its new asset. Occasionally, it will not be possible to persuade an agent to take money in return for his or her services; social position, pride, and a lack of need all can be factors in such a refusal. In that case, a scholarship for a child, a new car, or whatever else might be acceptable and valuable can be given as "gifts" to cement a relationship with a source. Boxes of fine cigars, in particular, seem to have an almost universal acceptability.

In the end, the case officer developing a potential recruit must make some basic decisions about the target. He and his superiors must most basically decide whether the final recruitment appeal or "pitch" can be made on the basis of perceived mutual interests—whether friendship, ideology, or perhaps the source's emotional dependence on the case officer will be a sufficient incentive for the acceptance of the recruitment offer—or if money or other material rewards will have greater appeal. The service always prefers to have *some* money involved in the recruitment and employment of a source for the reason given above, and some sources are mercenary in the fullest sense—that is, they "work" only for money. There have been a number of examples of such agents in recent years, as it is typical among the "small fry" found in the pool of those who have access to the information needed.

RECRUITMENT: THE SOFT SELL

"I thought you'd never ask . . . " Sound familiar? It should. After all, this is the way human relationships normally reach a state of fruition. This is the way that the process of recruitment of an agent should ideally reach a climax. The process of developing an identified potential agent should last for whatever time is necessary to create the rapport between the case officer and the agent. Ideally, it should almost never be necessary to ask the question, "Will you work for us?" In a typical scene, two people are playing golf or tennis with no one else present, and one turns to the other and says, "There is something that I and my people want to ask you to do." The other answers, "I thought you'd never ask." A recruitment attempt of that kind is the solidest sort of long-term arrangement, for the recruitment is based in trust, mutual regard, and shared values. In some cases, it may be necessary to bring in a specialist case officer who is known as a highly successful recruiter. This may be done if there is some doubt about the receptivity of the potential source to an appeal from the case officer who did the "development"—because, for example, the case officer is younger than the potential agent, or the case officer is a woman working with an agent from a culture that does not accept the idea of senior-subordinate relationships in which women are the supervisors. In many of these cases, the developmental work can be done well by a female case officer, but recruitment and subsequent management and control of the agent must be given to another. This may seem unfair to

Fulfilling Needs

Readers of "espionage fiction" may believe that some sort of magical hypnotism is involved in the process of recruiting agents that makes a "target" accept recruitment despite his or her better judgment and through the sheer force of the recruiting case officer's personality. This is almost never true. What really happens in most cases is that the "spotter" recognizes in a prospect a need to be accepted or to work toward the fulfillment of some deeply felt goal and then sets out to make the prospect believe that recruitment is the key to satisfying that need. Once the espionage unit has developed the relationship sufficiently for the prospect to *believe* that his or her need(s) will be met, "formal" recruitment becomes just that—a formality.

the case officer who executed the development, but it must be remembered that the public good is the only possible justification for activities of this kind and that personal considerations must not be a priority in making such decisions.

RECRUITMENT: THE HARD SELL

"Let's talk turkey." It sometimes becomes clear during development that the potential source, though reluctant to discuss the politics of "what should be done" about the problem or situation being used as a motivator, *is* susceptible to arguments that would "sell" the recruitment. If the source routinely "changes the subject" when the case officer tries to "lead" discussions into useful and suggestive areas, then it is soon evident that fear or some other inhibitor exists in the mind that is stronger than the officer's soft-sell appeals. In that case, the operations planning staff of the espionage team may decide to use the "hard sell." This means that, instead of speaking sweetly to the prospective source in the same way that he has been spoken to during the process of development, the officer must now speak in a demanding, even harsh way, summoning the source to "face up to his responsibilities" as a citizen and a human being and to "shoulder" the burden of doing this dangerous thing—either because it is his duty or because he has no choice. Coercion sometimes is the only way the recruitment can be made. Most often this comes in the form of an implied or even overt threat of disclosure of the prospective agent's previous help or of the gifts the source has already accepted from the espionage service. In the course of development, the case officer tries to get the source to begin to give him information. Usually, this begins with requests for readily available information in the "public domain" that seems to be innocuous. If the source performs this task well, then the "ante" is steadily "upped," with more and more information being sought, information of greater and greater sensitivity. If the source has done all this, then at the moment of crisis the case officer can remind him or her that the compromise has already taken place and can be revealed.

In any event, the source's acceptance of recruitment and a subordinate status *vis à vis* the espionage group is the goal. Once this is established, the espionage controllers may actually require the source to sign a contract of employment, either in true name or under a pseudonym. This is sought because the espionage unit wants the source to cross the emotional barrier of accepting his or her status as a committed member of the unit "team."

6

The Operational Cycle: Missions and Tradecraft

TRAINING FOR A MISSION

Once the prospective agent has "signed on the dotted line" and can be considered an asset of the espionage agency, then his training must begin. This training usually takes place in a facility known as a "safe house," a house or apartment or some other place that is under the complete control of the espionage service and believed to be unknown to adversaries and the general public. A lot of specialized training is required to make someone who has been successfully recruited into a dependable agent whose word can be relied on and who will obey his controllers. Such training is always "tailored" to the agent's particular task and reflects his status as a "property" of the espionage unit. It must be remembered that the agent is not a member of the espionage unit. He is, in fact, the unit's *servant*—and, as such, is expendable in a way that "staff members" of the intelligence service itself would never be. Some intelligence agencies feel a great deal of loyalty toward agents who serve them well and will try to ensure their welfare, but others are quite ruthless about discarding people who prove to be unreliable or useless. Agents are sometimes abandoned in the midst of operations, but more commonly they are "paid off" after failed missions to make their silence likely. This statement does not imply the possibility of the "extreme prejudice"—that is, murder—so favored by Hollywood. What it does imply is that enough money and job security will be found for the source to ensure that source's silence.

TRADECRAFT

Tradecraft is a "term of art" widely known in the espionage trade. It encompasses all the minutiae of operational method and art that have been collected by millennia of clandestine operators as the best ways of "running" agents in hostile environments. This chapter aims to outline some of the key elements of tradecraft; these are points of the spy's art whose mastery can mean the difference between success and failure—life and death.

Communications

This term covers a multitude of different aspects of training and operations. The means by which an espionage agency communicates with its committed agents who are operating in "enemy" territory are the most vulnerable parts of the whole plan of operations. This is true because the agent, when "hiding" inside the "disguise" of his normal, natural "cover," is very hard for the foreign counterintelligence services to identify and apprehend. It is only when the agent does things outside the pattern of his normal daily life or has to reach out to contact his controllers to report or receive instructions that he becomes a moving target, someone much more likely to attract the attention of those hunting his kind. It is therefore important for the agent and the service to have ways of

---

Training Agents in a Denied Area

The training of a new espionage agent is often carried out under remarkably difficult conditions. If the new agent is located in his own country in what is often called a "denied area," then it may be necessary to conduct training in short sessions in a "safe house" within this hostile and potentially disastrous environment. Police detection of a "disappearance" of the agent from public view is the most threatening aspect of training behind enemy lines. The preferred solution to the problem of security during training is to "exfiltrate" the agent to friendly and secure territory where the environment can be controlled more effectively. Business trips, vacations, and the like provide opportunities for this "exfiltration."

meeting and signaling with messages to each other that are least likely to attract enemy attention. For these reasons, a great deal of rather "spooky" business goes on in tradecraft.

Meetings

A meeting requires that the agent and a controlling case officer from the espionage unit be physically located in the same place at the same time. This is particularly difficult to arrange in security once the agent is placed inside the "denied area," the area in which his objective is located. The setup is inherently insecure, and one might fairly ask why one would do this at all.

The answer really lies in basic human nature. People need the solace of the real presence of their own kind. This is particularly true of human agents isolated among the enemy because of the nature of their "cover for status," which necessarily places them continuously among their enemies. Although it is possible to use other means of communication to agents, personal meetings will always be needed. Agents who cannot be reached for such meetings because of the tightness of enemy security tend to decline over time in morale and motivation to carry out the mission. If left to themselves long enough, such agents may simply come to view themselves as no longer being recruited assets of the espionage unit. This is very dangerous, for a "lost" agent may decide through remorse at having betrayed his friends to "return to the fold" and betray, in turn, the espionage team that has been running him.

To arrange a meeting, the "handler" has the problem of some-how signaling to his agent his desire for the meeting, along with such details as place, time, security arrangements, and so on. This is often done through the simple expedient of instructions given at the end of an earlier meeting. Such instructions often give the agent the details of how he will be signaled for a meeting or how he can signal for a meeting. At times, meetings are scheduled in great detail; at other times, they are left unscheduled, to be called as circumstance requires. To signal for an *unscheduled* meeting, a typical device would be to place marks on agreed-to landmarks, such as trees, post boxes, or rocks. The agent and the case officer both routinely check previously established locations for such signaling marks. When one or the other sees one, he or she makes an answering mark on a different tree or lamppost to show that the message has been received. The meeting then takes place at the appointed time and place.

Because face-to-face meetings can be very hard to arrange, a "brush pass" is often substituted. In this technique, an agent and a "handler" move past each other in some public place and, with minimal contact, one passes to the other some common object, such as a folded newspaper, that contains a coded message.

Live Drops and Dead Drops

Security concerns often make it inadvisable to arrange a meeting during which messages can be passed or the agent can report on his or her mission. In these situations, "live drops" or "dead drops" are used instead. Live drops use "post boxes" maintained and serviced by some cooperating party—ordinarily, a recruited "support agent" who is brought into the operation to perform this function. Dead drops are more complex; in general, they involve a hiding place in which messages are left but which is not checked consistently or spontaneously by any third party. The "drop site" in a dead drop can be any neutral element of the landscape, modified or unmodified, such as a hole in a wall or a hollow stone. These sites are scouted in advance and agreed to by both parties. When they are to be used, signal marks are left to alert the other party to go to the drop site to retrieve the message. Often the message is hidden in a "concealment device," which may be something like a hollow brick or a soft-drink can with a false bottom.

Invisible Ink

When messages are left at such drop sites or are sent through the postal mail, it is necessary to conceal the meaning of the text of the message from the possibility of interception by hostile counter-intelligence agencies or police. This is done through "secret writing."

This technique uses fluids such as blood, urine, and lemon juice (at the most basic level) to write the true messages between the lines of a "cover" letter or other document. When dry, these fluids fade to invisibility and can be "recovered" through the simple application of heat as a developer. There are also much more complex chemical "invisible inks," but these are the property of specific governments and do not work any better than the simple ones.

Photography

Spies take pictures. They don't like to do it, but they do it nonetheless. Why do they not want to do it? Because cameras raise questions. To carry a camera openly is to invite onlookers to ask *why*—Why is this person carrying a camera? Is he or she a tourist? To carry a *miniature* camera is to invite suspicion as a spy. To take pictures of important subjects—you get the idea. So, why carry or use a camera? One answer lies in the limits of human memory and trust. Human beings can remember only so much, and the fine detail that an intelligence analyst needs to see to comprehend the target is beyond most people's capacity for memorization.

Another reason why an agent would take pictures (at the direction of a handler) is the need to have the proof of accomplishment of a mission. Agents are always under suspicion of fabrication. They must be. If they are not, then their information lacks the rigorous proof of its validity that makes it valuable. Anyone who has seen the 1959 film production of the Graham Greene story "Our Man in Havana" knows the tale: A British man recruited to be a resident spy in Havana makes up his reports as exaggerations of the vacuum cleaner parts he sold in his shop. In his drawings, the various vacuum hoses, couplings, and tanks are blown up to thirty or forty feet in height and became the rocket base from which Florida could be bombarded. Such things *do* happen. They happen often, and for that reason agents are tested and retested for reliability. This makes it very desirable to be able to actually see the product of an agent's work, and this in turn makes photography worthwhile.

Countersurveillance

An agent lives with the constant fear that he has become an "object of interest" to the foreign equivalent of the American FBI. The agent seeks safety in anonymity and within the "ordinariness" of his daily routine. As long as he does nothing that breaks the pattern of his usual life, he is unlikely to attract attention; but his secret life makes it impossible *not* to break his normal pattern of activity, and this exposes him to danger. Meetings and the "servicing" of "dead drops" are two of the most dangerous events in his second life, and both present opportunities for someone, anyone, to see him doing something "strange" and report him to the police. To minimize the chance that he will be noticed, he learns to perform what is known as "countersurveillance." This is the skill of detecting anyone who follows him in the street, either in a car or on foot. Occasionally, one person conducts police surveillance, but this is often ineffective; the presence of one surveillant physically following the agent down the street is inherently easy to detect because the same face is always there, "tagging along" behind. More often, police surveillance usually consists of a team of three, four, or five people accompanying the agent on the street while trying to look inconspicuous and unremarkable. They "follow" the agent in a formation with some ahead, some in a parallel street, and someone behind. In a nearby van they will typically have backup surveillants ready to be put on the street to replace anyone who is judged to be "burned" or "made" by the quarry.

For the agent, surveillants present a number of problems. He must always be vigilant, and he must follow the detection techniques taught him by his handlers whenever he is doing something risky. He also must never appear to be conducting countersurveillance. It would (obviously) be incriminating for a supposedly innocent man to go to some lengths to detect police surveillance. Finally, he must never try to "lose" his followers. To do so would be the ultimate in *de facto* admission of his involvement in some activity that needs to be hidden.

To get all this right is a difficult business, but it is extremely necessary. If an agent or case officer detects surveillance during the approach to a meeting, the meeting is canceled immediately. Caution and a certain unwillingness to take risks are character- istics of long-lived espionage people, whether "staff" or agents. As an old saying of the espionage services goes, "There are old spies and there are bold spies, but there are no old, bold spies."

Debriefing and Reports

Whether it be in face-to-face meetings or through other means of communication, the espionage service receives information from its agents in response to the tasking that it has given them. With this information in hand, the service "sits down" to evaluate the information to determine two things about it: its credibility and its accuracy.

First: Is the source or chain of sources credible? In other words, does the service know enough about the person or persons who provided the information to be able to state to the consumer that it believes these sources to be dependably truthful? Because the service knows its own agent, it has the ability to "test" him or her intensively and repeatedly to uncover deception, or "paper milling," as the espionage community calls it. These tests can be varied in kind. Agents are sometimes sent to collect information concerning targets that are already well-known to the espionage service; the object of tests of this kind is to see whether the agent returns with information that agrees with that which is already known. Another commonly used technique for testing agents is simply to use the polygraph (lie detector) to find indications of deception. This device does not, in fact, determine truthfulness, but it *does* measure physiological indicators of stress in response to questions about the agent's truthfulness, etc. In the hands of a skilled operator, the polygraph has a high probability of success in revealing deception. The issue of the unacceptability of evidence derived from the polygraph in American courts is not pertinent in this use, because the agent is not the subject of a legal proceeding and this use for testing is entirely a matter of operational security.

The second question the recruiting organization must ask is equally fundamental: Does the service judge the information itself to be correct in its factual details? This is the more difficult of the two tasks, for, while the espionage service can control the recruitment and testing of its agents, it has no control over the analysts who are needed to provide a judgment about the correctness of the data itself. As a result, the espionage unit often has to go to intelligence programs outside the espionage group to solicit an opinion. This is inherently a difficult thing to do, because the analysts have a lot of work to do and writing evaluations of espionage reports usually is not a priority.

Retirement of Agents

Every espionage service hopes that its recruited foreign agents will survive in service so long that their help is no longer needed because of changing circumstances. The Hollywood-inspired myth that espionage services dispose of useless agents ruthlessly is completely false. Every effective espionage service in the world knows that, if it betrays its recruited agents, the "word" will quickly spread along the mysterious "jungle telegraph" of rumor that ties together the world of intelligence. If this happens, the responsible service will find that no other service or, indeed, no well-informed individual will want to have anything to do with it.

What really happens is that the service plans for the retirement of the agent from the time that he or she is recruited. In many instances, a portion of the "pay" due to the agent from the service is set aside in an "escrow account" against the day of the agent's retirement. This "escrow account" grows incrementally throughout the agent's service and is held for the agent in an interest-bearing account in a suitable and trustworthy bank. When retirement comes, the money belongs to the agent to help start a new life, perhaps in his original homeland or, more rarely, in the espionage service's country. This is called "resettlement," and because of additional costs, it is usually reserved for agents whose service has been so important that it is judged to be deserved.

7

The Future
of HUMINT

Is "spying" a good idea? Is it useful? Is it moral?

In an age of satellite photography and collection of enemy signal communications from outer space, one can logically ask whether it is really still necessary to use spies in foreign policy and military operations.

The answer is that it *is* still necessary.

Clandestine HUMINT—spying—provides an ability to see into the intentions of an adversary that no other form of intelligence collection can offer. SIGINT, the collection of enemy communications, can often give real insights into what the enemy would like to do, but this insight is always partial at best because the parties communicating may not themselves have a complete understanding of the situation and therefore may give the "listeners" an incorrect impression of enemy plans. A spy in the enemy's ministry of war who brings to his masters the complete plan of campaign of an aggressor even before war begins provides an insight that is beyond price. The ability to anticipate an adversary's "moves" and to counter them without great difficulty is invaluable and contributes directly to diplomatic efforts to avoid war or to a rapid victory with fewer casualties to all concerned.

The wars of the future are probably going to be wars in the "developing world," where seemingly obscure ideological movements and "rogue" rulers are likely to emerge as threats to world order and stability. Such wars will be seen by the great powers as "wars of liberation" waged on behalf of indigenous populations for the purpose of freeing the people from the bondage of tyrants and "backwardness." At the same time, dictators in the "Third World" will undoubtedly continue to try to develop or buy frightful weapons of mass destruction. Poison gas, diseases as weapons, and nuclear bombs are all tools of illegal warfare that some countries in Asia, Africa, and South America will continue to strive for.

In such wars waged in places with relatively primitive physical infrastructure in communications, highways, and urban facilities, the importance of tactical (battlefield) HUMINT can only grow. The ability of armed forces to recruit and successfully "run" agents who can report on troop movements and the plans of guerrilla commanders will be invaluable. Recent experience shows that in American forces, the CIA, U.S. Army, and Special Operations forces can effectively combine to insert case officers and commando observers into areas that are still under enemy control to bring near real-time information to commanders in the field with which to run a campaign in such a way as to preclude heavy loss of life.

At the same time, the existence of worldwide terrorist

Justifying Treason

The spy and his controller must face the dilemma of deciding for themselves if the betrayal of trust and duplicity inherent in espionage are justified by the greater good done by providing what they see as a just cause with the information needed in order to prevail. For those agents who are solely motivated by money, this is not an issue; but most agents are motivated by complex needs and fears that drive them to accept participation in activities that they would normally avoid. The most common reason for spying for a foreign entity is a belief that the foreign country will bring "freedom," "liberation," or "justice" to one's own people. Against such a motivational background, it is often easy to justify treason.

groups such as Al Qaeda shows the clear need to "penetrate" these groups so that their targeting and plans can be known. If the intentions of such groups are known, then they can be blocked in advance and tragedies like the attacks on New York and Washington will be prevented.

Are espionage operations *moral*? Is the manipulation of human motivations and needs ever justifiable? Each of us must answer this question as a matter of personal responsibility, but the arithmetic of the situation seems clear. Roughly three thousand people died in the terrorist attacks on New York and Washington. Saddam Hussein killed millions in his wars and during his reign of police terror. Would it not have been "moral" to prevent these outcomes by bringing a few individuals to accept their duty in helping to prevent such evil?

THE PROBLEM OF TERRITORIALISM AMONG AGENCIES

In just about every country in the world, there are at least two intelligence agencies. These agencies usually represent the civilian and military sides of the government. They usually regard each other with suspicion, and a deep-seated rivalry normally exists between them. This rivalry is a product of the innate competition for power and budgetary support (money) that exists among departments in every government. This competition is particularly counterproductive in the espionage function of a government, for the various intelligence groups are skilled in what the Soviet intelligence services called "conspiratorial work" and are adroit at undercutting one another and undermining one another's reputations. At times, they have been known to actually "sabotage" other departments' operations by claiming prior proprietary rights to an individual agent or by some other destructive stratagem. Such rivalries are serious problems, and many solutions have been suggested to this fundamental flaw in organization.

One of the most often suggested is simple amalgamation of all such agencies into one civilian service. This is appealing on the surface of the matter, but to do this would be to deprive the armed forces of the country of the specialized capability they need to work against specifically military targets. There is also the well-demonstrated fact that military officer targets are more easily recruited by other officers and not by civilians. These factors, taken together, have made for effective arguments against amalgamation as a solution.

In the absence of amalgamation of the services, the solution most often advocated has been closer coordination of the agencies under the supervision of a central authority. This seems like a good idea, but, in the United States, it has been tried as a solution for decades and has not worked well. The problem has been that the "coordinating authority" is the director of Central Intelligence (the DCI), who is also the director of the Central Intelligence Agency. The "wearing of two hats" by this one person has all too often resulted in the process of "coordination" of activities and operations being skewed in favor of the CIA. This does not really improve relations between the groups.

If there is a solution to this problem of "turf battles" among intelligence groups, it has not yet been found.

8

Entering the Field

Is espionage intelligence a profession, a trade, or just a job? Can a viable career exist in the field of HUMINT? These are valid questions, especially for anyone who may be thinking of future employment in the government of his country.

It seems obvious that a clandestine case officer is a professional in the truest sense of the word. His vocation requires a deep understanding of humankind, an instinctive "feel" for human motivation and needs. This understanding must be so profound that it is instinctual, *intuitive*. Intuition is really a reflexive and high-speed process of reasoning— reasoning so fast that the individual steps cannot be readily separated for inspection. The case officer must possess intuitive and "bone-deep" comprehension of how people function under stress. He must have knowledge of his skills so deep that this knowledge becomes an unthought-of capability. Whether such skills are innate or can be taught is arguable; certainly, some people are born with or raised to have many of the attributes needed for this kind of work, and in others those attributes can be developed. Unfortunately, there are individuals for whom the work of espionage is an incomprehensible and unwelcome task. There are many worthwhile endeavors in life, and not everyone is suited to them all.

Taking all this into account, what sort of education is optimal for the development of the clandestine operative? What sort of educational background will allow him to do his work successfully and with a detachment that does not lead, in the end, to the "Lawrence of Arabia" syndrome? T.E. Lawrence, the legendary British intelligence operative of World War I, could not live with his belief that he and the British Empire had betrayed and exploited his Arab friends by taking the lands that had been promised to them in return for their armed assistance to the Allies against Turkey. He spent the rest of his short life doing "penance" for what he saw as a personal moral failure. He is an unfortunate example of a case officer who "fell in love" with his agents, in this case, an entire people. His unhappy life ended in a motorcycle crash into a stone wall.

It is obvious that training in the necessary mechanics of the trade of espionage would be an essential part of the background of a successful clandestine operator. Clandestine communication, compartmentalization, spotting, assessing, and most importantly recruiting are all among the skills lumped together as "tradecraft." They are the bare bones, the skeleton of knowledge underlying the flesh of a competent clandestine operator. The clandestine

The Case Officer

The essence of any successful espionage effort lies in the empathic skills of the "case officer" or "agent handler." A highly skilled case officer once remarked that to be good at the job, an operative must be comfortable and able to function everywhere and in every setting. "From the locker room to the boardroom," was his formulation, and he was one the greatest "recruiters" that American intelligence has ever seen. A really successful case officer must be a true "Renaissance" person with a wide knowledge of history, psychology, literature, anthropology, and languages. Athletic and musical ability are also very helpful. The great irony of the craft of espionage is that in order to be really good at his job, a case officer must empathize deeply with his agent, must feel his joys and most profound fears and hopes; that is the only way he can truly control the agent. But at the same time, he must manipulate those feelings to accomplish the task at hand. It is difficult to say whether it is the agent or the case officer who is wounded more in the process.

services of every major country have training establishments that impart the kind of skills that are lumped together as "tradecraft" with varying emphasis in accordance with the history, experience, and national "taste" of the country involved.

It is arguably true that clandestine intelligence is an essential and indispensable part of the life of governments. Certainly, the record seems to indicate that it is inevitable. It is certainly true that it has been a feature of the "game of nations" for as long as humans have had governments. It is at least as old as diplomacy as a constant in history and probably not much different in time of origin from the soldier's vocation. Nevertheless, it is treated as a kind of afterthought by governments. There is no professional educational preparation for such a career, although the career itself is always with us. The soldier's vocation has ancient schools of professional education. The diplomat has his as well in programs like the School of Foreign Service at Georgetown. What is missing from the "vocation" of life in the clandestine services is an educational program analogous to West Point and Georgetown.

What kinds of things should be studied in such a program? Some thoughts:

- **Psychology.** The eighteenth-century English poet Alexander Pope wrote, "The proper study of Mankind is Man." This is most true in the case of the clandestine officer. Empathy and understanding of motivation are the keys to success.

- **Languages.** If you cannot readily converse with a subject, the game is half lost.

- **Law.** Specifically, the elements of law that apply to this field.

- **Anthropology.** A deep comprehension of the roots of behavior in a particular culture is all-important to success.

- **Economics.** For obvious reasons.

- **History** in general and **the history of intelligence** in particular. The record of man's existence is a guide to what he can be expected to do. Case studies of successful operations would yield comprehension of how to approach specific cases.

- **Philosophy.** The clandestine officer must be a person of intellectual weight to gain respect.

- **Athletics.** *Mens sana in corpore sano*—in other words, "a healthy mind in a healthy body."

- **Basic science and mathematics.** The real world is filled with technology; one must comprehend this or be irrelevant.

- **Literature.** See **Philosophy**.

A program like this would focus on the humanities in general and the liberal arts in particular, for the proper business of the clandestine operator is the understanding of humans themselves. Engineers, accountants, and scientists do not normally make good clandestine officers. Their focus in life is on things not people. Such folk are best involved in clandestine operations as consultants in targeting and debriefing and not in the inner "mysteries" of espionage's humanist heart.

Is there a university with the courage and dedication to create such a program? Perhaps there will be, someday.

"The proper study of Mankind is Man."

—Alexander Pope (1688–1744),
"An Essay on Man"

Andrew, Christopher. *The Sword and the Shield: The Mitrokhin Archive.* Basic Books, 1999. [This is the British intelligence–sponsored publication of part of the KGB archive stolen by Mitrokhin.]

Bennett, Richard M. *Espionage: An Encyclopedia of Spies and Secrets.* Virgin Books, 2002. [Another encyclopedic work.]

Gertz, Bill. *Breakdown: How America's Intelligence Failures Led to September 11.* Regnery Publishing, 2002. [Bill Gertz is a military writer for *The Washington Times.* This is his book on the failures in HUMINT of American intelligence.]

Klehr, Harvey, and John Earl Haynes. *Venona: Decoding Soviet Espionage in America.* Yale University Press, 1999. [This book describes the results of "decrypting" Soviet intelligence communications.]

Klehr, Harvey, John Earl Haynes, and Fridrikh Igorevich Firsov. *The Secret World of American Communism.* Yale University Press, 1995. [This fascinating book was written with the cooperation of Russian officials. It describes in detail the assistance given to Soviet intelligence by the underground branch of the American Communist Party.]

Shulsky, Abram N., and Garry J. Schmitt. *Silent Warfare: Understanding the World of Intelligence.* Brassey's, 2002. [An encyclopedic basic work.]

Tanenhaus, Sam. *Whittaker Chambers.* The Modern Library, 1997. [Chambers was a courier for the GRU in the 1930s and was a key witness against Alger Hiss.]

Tidwell, William A. *Come Retribution: The Confederate Secret Service and the Assassination of Lincoln.* University of Mississippi Press, 1988. [The definitive work on Confederate intelligence involvement in the murder of Lincoln. The author knew Tidwell.]

Vagts, Alfred. *The Military Attaché.* Princeton University Press, 1967. [The most complete description ever written of the work of a military attaché.]

Weinstein, Allen, and Alexander Vassiliev. *The Haunted Wood: Soviet Espionage in America: The Stalin Era.* Random House, 1999. [Another excellent work written from KGB files on the successes of the NKVD in the United States.]

CNN: Cold War Experience: Espionage
www2.cnn.com/SPECIALS/cold.war/experience/spies/
An entertaining and informative online exhibition of espionage-related material, especially pertaining to the Cold War.

The National Security Archive
www.gwu.edu/~nsarchiv/NSAEBB/NSAEBB46/
An independent nonprofit organization, housed at George Washington University, that collects declassified government documents. An extremely rich source of information on many topics related to American national security.

DEBKAfile: Political Analysis, Espionage, Terrorism Security
www.debka.com
This Israeli site, published in both English and Hebrew, is a rich "lode" of (sometimes) accurate information.

The Washington Post: Espionage
www.washingtonpost.com/wp-dyn/nation/nationalsecurity/spying/
Offers an archive of dozens of articles on current events in the field of espionage. An ideal source of information on stories currently in the news.

The Federation of American Scientists: Intelligence Resource Program: "An Assessment of the Aldrich H. Ames Espionage Case and Its Implications for U.S. Intelligence"
www.fas.org/irp/congress/1994_rpt/ssci_ames.htm
A complete account of this disaster in American national security.

University of Michigan: School of Information: Spy Letters of the American Revolution
www.si.umich.edu/spies/
A fascinating online exhibition of correspondence among spies during the American Revolution. The site covers methods of communicating secretly, modes of transporting the letters, and the stories of some of the spies themselves.

The Cato Institute: Policy Analysis: "Why Spy?: The Uses and Misuses of Intelligence"
www.cato.org/pubs/pas/pa-265.html
A heavily documented scholarly work that criticizes what it considers the Clinton administration's pursuit of economic espionage. The Cato Institute is a respected nonprofit organization based in Washington, D.C., that aims to strengthen the link between "the intelligent, concerned lay public" and government decision making.

U.S. Army Intelligence Center and Fort Huachuca: "Masters of the Intelligence Art: Grenville M. Dodge and George H. Sharpe: Grant's Intelligence Chiefs in the West and East"
138.27.35.32/History/PDFS/MDODGE.PDF
The part of this document that deals with Colonel Sharpe, Grant's Chief of Intelligence, is invaluable. The main site (*138.27.35.32*) offers links to several highly educational sites on military intelligence in subdomains such as history and training.

page:

i:	© Bettmann/CORBIS	v:	© Bettmann/CORBIS
ii:	© CORBIS	vi:	© Bettmann/CORBIS
iii:	© Bettmann/CORBIS	vii:	© Bettmann/CORBIS
iv:	Associated Press, AP	viii:	Associated Press, AP/Bob Daugherty

Colonel W. Patrick Lang is a retired senior officer of U.S. Military Intelligence and U.S. Army Special Forces (the Green Berets). He served in the Department of Defense for many years, both as a serving officer and, later, as a member of the Defense Senior Executive Service. He is a highly decorated veteran of several of America's overseas conflicts, including the war in Vietnam. He was trained and educated as a specialist in the Middle East by the U.S. Army and has served extensively in that region. He was the first Professor of the Arabic Language at the United States Military Academy at West Point, New York. In the Defense Intelligence Agency (DIA), he was the Defense Intelligence Officer for the Middle East, South Asia, and Terrorism, and later he became the first Director of the Defense HUMINT Service. For his service to the DIA, he was awarded the Presidential Rank of Distinguished Executive, the equivalent of a British knighthood. He is an analyst/consultant for many television and radio broadcasts, among them *The Jim Lehrer Newshour.*

Larry C. Johnson is a recognized expert in the fields of counterterrorism, aviation security, and crisis and risk management. He has worked with the CIA and served as Deputy Director of the U.S. State Department's Office of Counterterrorism. In addition to his many published articles and interviews on television and radio, he has designed counterterrorism "war games" and represented the U.S. government at the OSCE Terrorism Conference in Vienna in 1996. He has played a key role in counterterrorism operations in the Middle East. Mr. Johnson currently is the chief executive officer of BERG Associates, LLC, an international consulting firm that helps multinational corporations and financial institutions manage the risks and counter the threats posed by terrorism and money laundering.